The Beginner's Guide to

GREAT GOLF FOR WOMEN

GREAT GOLF

The BEGINNER'S GUIDE to

FOR WOMEN

VERNON

JUERGENS

with

RHONDA

GLENN

Taylor Publishing Company

Dallas, Texas

Published by Taylor Publishing Company
        1550 West Mockingbird Lane
        Dallas, Texas 75235

All photographs by Willis Knight.
Our thanks to Alison Hayden, Ernie Coleman, DeAnna Doud, and Marlena Jones for posing for these photographs.
Designed by David Timmons

Library of Congress Cataloging-in-Publication Data
Juergens, Vernon.
    The beginner's guide to great golf for women / Vernon Juergens
  with Rhonda Glenn.
      P.   cm.
    ISBN 0-87833-853-5
    1. Golf for Women. I. Glenn, Rhonda. II. Title.
GV966.J84   1993
796.352—dc20   93-42903
                                          CIP

Printed in the United States of America
10 9 8 7 6 5 4 3 2 1

To my family, friends, students, and those whose loyalty has been constant. We have traveled the world, and the memories of playing golf, both nationally and internationally, have been a lifetime of pleasure.

The extensive growth in golf will be among women players. They make up seventy-seven percent of today's golf market; over five million women play golf. In the last five years, forty percent of the new golfers have been women. It is predicted that women will make up half of the golfing population by the year 2000. It is to this growing group of golfers that this book is also dedicated.

May this book add to your accomplishments. Whether you're just beginning or seeking to improve, I wish you a lifetime of enjoyment.

VERN JUERGENS

Contents

Introduction

Golf, a game once reserved for royalty and the wealthy, has become a game available to nearly everyone. One only has to read about the constant need for new golf courses to realize the game's exceptional appeal.

Of course, every player wants to play par golf. However, we must first honestly evaluate ourselves—our athletic ability and the amount of time we can allot to both practice and actual play—before we set our goals.

This book is designed specifically for women because they encounter different problems in golf than men. Because private clubs and public courses were originally organized for men, women are now faced with the difficulty of establishing their role in the world of golf. This is true for women who are striving to be superior golfers, social golfers, or golfers who compete in local tournaments.

Although practice and competition are important, it is equally important for beginning women golfers to enjoy the pleasure of the game. I have seen women throughout the United States, from all backgrounds, enjoy making golf their game. Some are from rural areas, others are from cities; some are serious athletes, others are recreational players. All of these women, with occasional but not grueling practice, have the potential to hit the ball very well and play an enjoyable game of golf.

Many women golfers learn a basic grip, and that's about all. From there, they develop their own unique swings and, surprisingly, learn to hit the ball quite well—without much practice.

Although women have special problems, they also have a special place in golf. I don't agree with the theory that a woman's game suffers because she lacks the muscular development of a man. To study the success of opposing muscle structures, we need only to look at the diminutive Chi Chi Rodrigues as opposed to the muscular Jim Thorpe. They're both great players. How can Chi Chi hit the ball as far as other senior pros and yet be so small? Gary Player, Ben Hogan, and Dave Marr are examples of smaller players of the past who became great international golfers. Jeff Sluman is an example of a contemporary golfer who is not overly muscular yet can hit the ball as far as almost anyone.

In the past, the majority of women were discouraged from athletics. Those who chose to develop their athletic talents were often labeled "tomboys." Most of the good women players, like Babe Zaharias and Patty Berg, excelled at other sports. And, among modern players, England's Laura Davies can hit the ball as far as many men professionals. Unfortunately, these women were too often the exception to the rule. Today's woman golfer can enjoy the same opportunities as the man golfer of the past.

My intention is not to examine various calibers of players but to examine muscular power, which is often misunderstood. Muscular power doesn't necessarily generate from sheer muscle mass. Powerful movements in the golf swing can be subtle, but they must exist. They are developed through practice.

If anything, it is a golfer's athletic talent and intensity that assure success. Women face difficulties that men do not. One of these difficulties is a woman's hip structure. Even the breasts can interfere with the traditional take-away and follow-through.

I have young women friends who lift weights. At first, I found this totally foreign, that is, until I discovered that women can use modified weight lifting, which tones muscles without building bulk, to strengthen the muscles used for golf. If a woman wants to be a great golfer, she'll need to exercise in many ways. In the past she was a tomboy, but today she is maintaining her health. Aerobics, bicycling, track, and many other sports are enjoying the impact of women. We have only to look at the incredible feats of athletes such as Janet Evans and Florence Griffith-Joyner to see the breakthroughs women are making in sports.

It is always rewarding to read about the great women golfers of the 1920s and 1930s, such as Joyce Wethered and Glenna Collett Vare. It's great players like these who took the "puff" shots out of women's golf. They played intensely; they swung hard.

Among more recent golfers, Babe Zaharias was possibly the greatest influence in getting women to strive for power. No doubt her background as an Olympic superstar in track-and-field events contributed to her wide-ranging influence.

Zaharias played her first game of golf at Bel-Air Country

Club in Beverly Hills, California. One of her competitors, Grantland Rice, participated in a small wager that even Babe couldn't play a decent round of golf. A local professional gave Babe a few basic instructions, and she proceeded to beat Grantland Rice *and* his cronies. What a story!

Let's address senior women golfers, those over fifty years of age. I belonged to a golf club in California where some of the women members in this age group had never played golf. They organized, asked a professional to help them, and became proficient golfers capable of playing with anyone. I admit they're not championship golfers nor will they win any local tournaments. They do, however, enjoy the beauty, freedom, sociability, and competitive spirit of golf. And believe me, as fast players women are well ahead of the field.

Women are certainly a major part of golf's enormous projected growth. But they must use their potential—their desire to play and their intensity—and have good reasons for wanting to play golf if they want to succeed. That's one of the greatest aspects of golf; whether you shoot in the 70s, 80s, 90s, or over 100, you can have fun no matter who your opponent is. Golf's handicapping system allows you to have a good match with anyone. (Your "handicap" is the average number over par that you usually score.) You can play at a level that will force your opponent to play to his or her own maximum ability. A scratch handicap golfer, a golfer with a zero handicap, feels just as badly losing to a 20- or 30-handicapper as losing to a player of his or her own ability.

Today, many teachers claim that their way is the only way to swing a golf club. College golfers and touring professionals alike often believe that their own swing is the only one that will succeed. Yet all of us can compete, even with an odd swing.

I have seen some people with seemingly terrible swings play good golf. There are even a few players who adjust their swings to compensate for physical disadvantages. One example is the young professional Jim Nelford who lost most of the muscles in his right arm and hand due to an injury.

For examples of odd swings, look to the men's senior tour. For some reason, no matter what the golf swing looks like, the clubhead comes through on the right plane, and they hit the ball the way players thirty years younger would like to.

Women's golf swings, aptitudes, and desires are unique. Still, all PGA and LPGA pros are competing and shooting low scores consistently. What can a woman golfer anticipate? What can she expect? How do women compete with men?

Women born before around 1965 were usually not encouraged to participate in sports. Such attitudes have, fortunately, changed, and women over the age of thirty can now develop their athletic ability.

This book addresses the problems and advantages that women golfers have. There's no doubt that the stamina of a woman is equal to that of a man. An example of this is women's participation in endurance sports such as cross country skiing and long distance running.

I would like to emphasize that this book is written to give women confidence in their abilities and help them learn how to play golf. Or, if they already play golf, it will give them more shots to work with. Ultimately, the intention is to help provide women with the basic skills to play better golf and, in the process, teach them the joys of the game.

All of us realize that problems and frustrations are endless when making a lifelong study of the game. But to overcome and solve those problems is a joy!

Golf does not exist exclusively for one race, one financial bracket, or one gender. It can, and does, appeal to everyone. Once a person is bitten by the golf bug, they're hooked for life. They love it not only because of the game and the competition but also because of its peace and beauty. All of these joys are available to women as well as men.

1.

. . . .

Learning the Lingo

I won't assume that everyone knows how to play golf. Although there may be a few veteran golfers among you, most of you are just becoming interested in learning. Before we can proceed with your lessons, you need to know how the game is played.

The object of the game is to strike the ball with a club and to get the ball into the hole in the fewest possible number of strokes. The completion of eighteen holes is considered a "round" of golf. This chapter contains some of the important terms in golf's vocabulary.

Golf Courses: You've all seen them, those beautiful stretches of carefully manicured grass, often lined with trees. There's usually a smattering of water and sand. Most golf courses have eighteen holes, but some are 9-hole courses. Private clubs, public courses, and resort courses sometimes have more than eighteen holes, but the courses are always laid out in groups of nine holes. A course, for instance, may have twenty-seven holes, or three "nines." It may also have thirty-six holes, or four nines. It may even have fifty-four holes, or six nines. Since a round of golf is the completion of eighteen holes, you play two nines to complete a round.

Front Nine and Back Nine: Holes one through nine are the "front nine," and holes ten through eighteen are the "back nine." Between holes nine and ten, or between the front and back nine, you make the "turn." On almost all courses the turn brings you back to the clubhouse. This is a good time to use the restroom and buy snacks or refreshments.

Parts of the Golf Course: A golf course consists of elements designed to give the course variety and make the game more challenging and fun. Play of each hole begins from a teeing area, or "tee." The tee is usually closely clipped grass and is identified by a set, or several sets, of tee markers. These markers are in pairs and are usually different colors. For example, one pair of markers may be red and another pair may be blue. The two markers in each pair are set far enough apart to provide a variety of places from which you can hit the ball.

The very front tee markers on each hole are called the "forward tees," and they mark the shortest version of the course. (Because these tees have traditionally been played by women, you may hear them called the "ladies' tees" but this is outdated.) The forward tees mark a course appropriate for women, junior, and senior golfers. However, some courses have a separate set of tee markers for senior players located between the forward and middle tees.

You'll play from the same set of tee markers for the entire round. Each course has its own "scorecard" that provides the length of the course from each tee and the distance from the tee to the center of the green for each tee on each hole. Some scorecards also have a picture of each hole. This is handy if you've never played the course before, because you can't always see the green from the tee.

As you advance in skill, you may want to move back to the next set of tee markers. On a course with no senior tees, these are called the "middle tees." These tees have traditionally been played by men (so you may hear the outdated term "men's tees" used for them), but they are also good for advanced women golfers.

The extreme back tee markers designate the longest version of the course and are called the "back tees." They are used by professionals and advanced men players. However, the most advanced women players occasionally play a round from the back tees for an added challenge.

Next, you'll encounter the "fairway." This is the preferred path to the end of the hole. It's a smoothly cut stretch of grass bordered on each side by higher grass. This higher grass is called the "rough."

At the end of each fairway is a "green." The green is an extremely smooth area of closely cut, well-manicured grass. On the green is the hole. In the hole is a pole with a flag on it—this is the "flagstick."

On the way from the tee to the hole, you'll see hollows filled with sand. These are "bunkers," or "sand traps." Try to avoid them, as you'll find that shots from bunkers can be very difficult.

You may also notice a few areas of water in the form of lakes, seas, ponds, rivers, or ditches. These are "water hazards." At all costs, avoid them. If you hit a ball into a water hazard, you'll not only suffer a penalty stroke, but you'll also more than likely lose your ball.

White stakes, or a white line, mark the outer limits of the course. These are "out-of-bounds stakes" or the "out-of-bounds line." You must stay within the limits of these markers to avoid being penalized.

Clubs: Golf is played with a maximum of fourteen clubs in one round. The club is composed of a "grip," "shaft," and "clubhead." Each clubhead has a number on it for identification. Clubs are designed for players of varying strengths and abilities. They come in different lengths and weights and with different shaft "flexes." (Flex refers to how much bend a shaft has.) It's always wise to consult a golf professional when purchasing clubs. The pro will help you find a suitable set for your build and skill level.

"Irons" have rather thin, almost knife-like, clubheads and are numbered one through nine. The lower the number of a club, the longer you can hit the ball when you use it. The 1-, 2, and 3-irons will hit the ball quite a long way. They're called the "long irons." The 4-, 5-, and 6-irons are used to hit the ball a medium distance, and they're your "middle irons." The 8- and 9-irons hit the ball only a short distance, and they're called "short irons."

Irons hit the ball varied distances because the front of each clubhead, called the "clubface," has a different degree of slope, or "loft." In other words, the angle of the clubface of a 1-iron has almost no loft. It will hit the ball on a low trajectory, which makes the ball go farther. Conversely, the clubface of the 9-iron is extremely lofted. It will hit the ball at a very high trajectory, and, because the ball goes so high, its momentum will be up instead of forward and the ball won't travel very far.

The rather massive clubheads of "woods" were once made almost exclusively of wood, and that's how they got their name. In recent years, many woods have been constructed with metal clubheads. However, we still refer to these clubs as woods.

Woods also have numbers on them. As with the irons, the lower the number, the lower the trajectory of the ball and the farther you can hit that club. A traditional set of woods for women includes a 1-wood, or a "driver." This is the club you use to hit the ball from a tee on most holes. You'll also have a 3-wood and possibly a 4-wood or a 5-wood; all hit the ball at a slightly higher trajectory and are good clubs to use when the ball is sitting on the grass. These are called "fairway woods." Woods are used for long shots; irons are used for accuracy.

Your "pitching wedge," an iron, has an even greater loft than your 9-iron. You'll use this club as you get closer to the hole. It's designed for accuracy and is an excellent club to use on short shots to the green.

The "sand wedge," also an iron, has the highest loft of any club and a very heavy clubhead. The clubhead also has a wide bottom, or "flange," on it. The flange will cause the clubhead to bounce when it comes in contact with the ground. That's why it's used to play out of bunkers—it won't dig into the sand and stop before you hit the ball. You may also find that it's a good club to use when playing short shots around the green.

Your "putter" is for use once your ball is on, or very near, the green; it is the most accurate of all clubs. It usually has a head made of steel, although many of the newer putters have heads made of some composite, even wood. The head of your putter is called the "putter head."

The face of the putter is almost completely vertical. This

means that when you stroke the ball it will stay on the ground and, hopefully, roll very smoothly into the hole.

The Scores: Each hole is designed to be played in a certain number of strokes; this number is called "par." If you score one stroke over par, you've made a "bogey." Two strokes over par is a double bogey, three shots over is a triple bogey, etc. If you score one stroke under par, you've made a "birdie." A score of two strokes under par is called an "eagle."

Other Equipment: You'll need a "golf bag" in which to carry your clubs. It has a strap and several pockets for carrying balls, tees, and other small items. Your golf bag is considered part of your equipment.

You'll also have a set of "headcovers"; they protect the heads of your woods. Some of the newer irons, those made of composites that can easily be scratched or damaged, also have small plastic protective covers.

Getting Around the Course: There are several modes of transportation in golf. Certainly the most invigorating way to play golf is to walk and carry your own bag. Some courses have caddies available, although caddying is a vanishing art form. A caddie will carry your clubs for you. Good caddies can also be invaluable advisers for determining the distance to the hole and helping the golfer "read the green," which means giving advice as to which directions a putt may "break," or roll. Caddies also rake bunkers, clean clubs, and do other things to aid the player. Nearly all modern golf courses also have motorized golf carts, pull carts, or both for rent. The pull cart permits the golfer to walk, pulling her clubs behind her. The motorized cart, which is now universally popular, carries two golfers and their clubs.

The Golf Shop: This shop, also called the "pro shop," is where you'll pay any charges associated with your day at the golf course. It's staffed by the golf professional and assistant professionals. This is the place you call to get a "tee time," the time you begin playing a round. To be sure that you get the tee time you want, it's best to call four or five days in advance.

You'll check in at the golf shop upon arriving and pay the fee for playing, which is called a "greens fee." At the same time, you'll arrange for your pull cart or golf cart or inquire about caddies. Caddies are paid at the end of the round, and most clubs specify a set caddie fee. It's not necessary to tip caddies; however, if you wish to, there's no set percentage. You may also want to purchase equipment or clothes, and most golf shops are well stocked with such merchandise.

The Practice Tee: This is a practice area, sometimes called a "driving range," where you can warm up for your round, practice, or take golf lessons. Inquire in the golf shop about practice facilities.

The Chipping Green and Putting Green: Most golf courses now have a chipping green for practicing chip shots, and many have an adjacent practice bunker. (Many courses designed before 1940 don't have chipping greens.) There is also a practice putting green where you can stroke a few putts to get the feel of the greens before playing.

2.

....

Preparing for Play

Years ago, when society was decidedly stodgy, women golfers were not allowed to play unless they wore skirts. However, women weren't the only ones who had to adhere to a dress code—men were once required to wear jackets, long-sleeved shirts, and ties. But the dress code has become relaxed, and by the 1950s women were allowed to play golf in Bermuda shorts as long as they were no shorter than knee length.

Today's golf clothes are more comfortable and colorful. Versatile, new easy-care fabrics have made the golf wardrobe casual. However, golf still maintains a dress code, and most courses require conservative dress. Short shorts, jeans, cut-offs, tight slacks, T-shirts, shirts without collars, and halter tops are not only inappropriate, they're usually not allowed. If you dress conservatively, however, you'll be welcome at any course.

Choose comfortable, rather loose-fitting golf clothes. Not only do they look nicer, but they'll also make it easier to swing the club and play well.

On warmer days, you'll do well to wear a cotton knit shirt with a collar or a short-sleeved cotton blouse that allows plenty of swing room. A nice pair of shorts with pockets for your tees and scorecard will also be appropriate.

On cooler days, slacks will do. Experienced golfers know to layer their clothes in cold weather by wearing a sweater or two. You can always shed the sweaters as the day warms up, but it's difficult to play well when you're chilled. It's also a good idea to keep a lightweight windbreaker in your bag for cool weather.

Most golfers become so addicted to the game that they'll even play in rain showers. (If you notice lightning when you're playing in the rain, take shelter immediately.) Knowing that golfers will play in the rain, clothing manufacturers have developed superior golf rainsuits. They're made of a fabric similar to that used for a windbreaker but waterproof. Be sure to purchase a rainsuit in a generous size; it must fit over your normal golf clothing and still provide plenty of room for you to swing comfortably. Don't forget to buy a good golf umbrella, too.

Many beginning golfers wear sneakers, and that's just fine. As you begin to play more, you'll want to invest in a pair of golf shoes. Golf shoes have spikes on the soles and provide much better traction when you're making a vigorous swing. They're also designed for walking and provide good support. Be sure to purchase golf shoes that fit properly and are not too tight. There's nothing more miserable than trying to finish a round when you have blistered feet.

I suggest that you invest in a golf glove. Many golf gloves have a small snap with a "ball marker"—this is used to mark the location of your ball on the green so that another player may putt. Golf gloves can be expensive, but they'll afford you a more secure grip on the club. You may also purchase a half-glove, which exposes the tips of your fingers but protects the palm and provides traction. Leather golf gloves are the most expensive, but they wear well and last a long time with proper care. Some glove manufacturers have developed new synthetics. These gloves are growing in popularity because they're durable and less costly than leather.

Right-handed golfers need a glove only for the left hand, and left-handed golfers need a glove only for the right hand. If your hands are extremely delicate, however, you may want to purchase a glove for each hand. Of course, there are some players, like Fred Couples, who don't wear a glove at all. You can choose what type of glove to buy and how many, if any, you want to wear. Always choose what is most comfortable.

This is an important warning: a round of golf usually means four or five hours in direct sunlight. Most of you know that sunlight will not only age your skin but can also be very dangerous because of the impact of harmful ultraviolet rays. Many golfers who have spent years in the sun with seemingly little effect are now discovering that they have developed skin cancer.

Newly released research indicates that even popular sunscreens aren't doing the job. Although dermatologists and sunscreen manufacturers have touted many sunscreens as means of preventing melanoma—the deadliest form of skin cancer—a July 1993 report in *The Proceedings of the National Academy of Sciences* says that most sunscreens do not provide protection from ultraviolet-a light rays. These rays, known as UVA, are the most dangerous. The report suggests that those who spend time in the sun use new sunscreens that specifically block UVA. It is also a good idea to purchase lip balm with UVA protection.

If you wipe perspiration from your face while playing golf, you may be removing your sunscreen. To be sure you're protected, apply a good waterproof UVA sunscreen to all exposed skin at least thirty minutes before you play. Don't forget the back of your neck, the tops of your ears, and the backs of your hands. Also keep in mind that women develop skin cancer on their legs more than any other part of their body.

Carry sunscreen in your bag and reapply it to exposed skin at least once while you're playing. After applying the sunscreen, wash or wipe it from the palms of your hands so they won't slip when you grip the club.

Wearing a hat also guards against the sun's rays. Combined with the use of sunscreen, a hat provides fairly good protection. A variety of golf hats are available. Many women wear visors. If you're purchasing one, look for a visor with a large bill for more protection. However, visors do not protect the top of your head or the back of your neck. For this reason, golfers are increasingly turning to wide-brimmed straw hats for more complete protection.

Experienced golfers, particularly those who live in the sunbelt, visit their dermatologists yearly. Suspicious skin lesions and precancerous sun conditions can, in most cases, be easily removed. Darkened spots with irregular borders and spots that increase drastically in size should be checked immediately.

Golf is generally a safe game. However, the increasing awareness of UVA means that a healthful-looking tan is no longer healthful—it's downright foolish and dangerous.

3.

Putting is Half
of the Game

Now for the fun—the exhilaration
of executing a good shot!

Most golf books save the chapter on putting for the end.
This book, written specifically for women, explains putting before any other golf shot. Many women are unfamiliar with what
it feels like to strike a ball. For the new golfer, learning to putt
properly will naturally lead to striking the ball properly on full
shots.

Putting properly is also a good way for advanced golfers
to improve their games. Veteran champion Kathy Whitworth is
among the number of premier players and instructors who

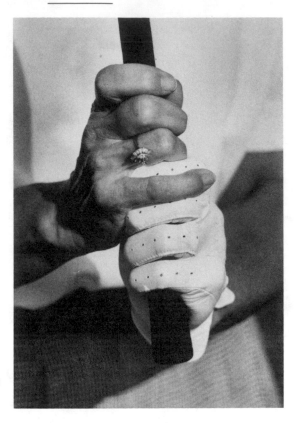

THIS IS A STANDARD VARDON GRIP. THE LITTLE FINGER OF THE RIGHT HAND OVERLAPS THE CLOSED SPACE BETWEEN THE FIRST TWO FINGERS OF THE LEFT HAND.

believe swing errors show up throughout one's game—from swinging the driver right down to the putting stroke.

All golfers, whatever their skill level, know that putting is at least half of scoring well. So, think of putting as the first step to building a fine all-around golf game.

First, you must learn to grip the golf club. (The grip described here is for right-handed players. Left-handed golfers should simply mirror, or reverse, the instructions.) Your grip is your only contact with the club. If you're using an incorrect grip, you'll make an equally incorrect adjustment in your putt to compensate. Unless you have unusually small hands or fingers, I recommend the Vardon grip. (More about the grip, including information on the interlocking grip and the baseball grip, will

be explained in detail in chapter 5.) In the Vardon grip, the little
finger of the right hand overlaps the closed space between the
first two fingers of the left hand. This grip may feel a little awkward at first, but it will begin to feel more comfortable after a
few practice sessions.

To grip your putter, simply stand with your arms hang-
ing down, then bring them together palm to palm. Don't alter
your elbows or go through contortions, we're seeking to guide
you to natural golf.

This palm-to-palm position is what you want when you
grip the putter. Using the Vardon grip, your left hand should be
the higher hand on the putter grip. With the back of your left
hand squarely facing your target, curl your fingers around the
grip, with your left thumb pointing down the top of the grip.
Slide your right hand down so it becomes the bottom hand.
Curl your fingers around the grip, and let the little finger of your
right hand overlap the index finger of your left hand. Your right
thumb should also point down the top of the grip. There should
be no space between your thumb and forefinger on either hand.

Preparing to Putt

First, we're going to work on putts of one to two feet in
length. After getting the proper grip, take your stance. The stance
should be a comfortable position with the knees slightly flexed.
Your feet should be aligned with the hole. To establish your "line,"
or the line on which you want your putt to roll, imagine that
you placed a yardstick on your toes and it continued in a line
parallel to the line to the hole.

Putting is a personal technique. Many good putters place
one foot or the other slightly forward. Other good putters hold

WHEN PREPARING TO GRIP YOUR PUTTER, STAND NATURALLY AND BRING YOUR HANDS TOGETHER AROUND THE PUTTER GRIP, PALM TO PALM. THEN TAKE YOUR GRIP.

WHEN PUTTING, YOUR STANCE SHOULD BE COMFORTABLE WITH YOUR
KNEES SLIGHTLY FLEXED. WHEN PRACTICING, PLACE A CLUB IN FRONT
OF YOUR FEET TO BE SURE THAT YOUR FEET ARE ALIGNED PARALLEL TO A
LINE FROM THE BALL TO THE HOLE.

ALL GOOD PUTTERS STAND WITH THEIR EYES DIRECTLY OVER THE BALL.

their elbows pointing out, or they may keep them tucked in. This is *your* decision and *your* experiment. Use whatever works best and most consistently for you.

All good putters do certain things alike. One is to stand with their eyes directly over the ball. Always be sure that your head is positioned so that your eyes are directly over the ball. Rest the putter head behind the ball with the face of the club pointing directly at your target.

The Putting Stroke

Take the putter back naturally. Don't use your hands to turn the clubface backward or forward, just take the putter straight back. Your arms (especially your left arm and hand) move straight back on the line of your putt.

Some great putters open or close the clubface upon striking the ball. I believe that it's better to take the putter back on a straight line without opening or closing the clubface.

On your forward stroke, stroke through the ball on your line with a slight upswing. In other words, the putter head will be traveling up slightly as you strike the ball.

This technique will put over-spin on the ball, helping it hold its line in case the green is rough or slow. Over-spin also helps you roll the ball through damage on the green that you're not allowed to repair, such as spike marks. Greens vary in speed. They can be very fast or very slow. Over-spin gives you an advantage on any type of green.

Here's a crucial point to remember on the putting stroke as well as on the full swing. *Your stroke must accelerate through the ball.* The acceleration will vary with the length of the putt. On a long putt, the acceleration of the clubhead through the ball is paramount. Your take-away should be slow, but your forward stroke *must* accelerate.

Ideally, the face of the putter remains square to its intended line on both the back stroke and the forward stroke. On the forward stroke, this is accomplished by keeping your left wrist frozen.

A key to good putting is to make sure that your stroke never crosses the line to the hole. When practicing, always establish your line and discipline yourself to stroke the ball along that line.

Putting is a quiet stroke. In other words, keep your body and head very still, very quiet. Use only your hands, arms, and shoulders.

After you've made several putts of one to two feet in length, try some three-foot putts. Don't think you are wasting time. If you're a good player, half of your shots will be on the putting green. The more proficient you become on the green, the lower scores you will shoot. Even a pro will tell you that putting is the basis of good scoring. As you begin making most of the three-foot putts, increase your distance from the hole.

When I lived in the Midwest, the ground was often covered with snow, so my youngest daughter practiced putting on the living room carpet. She became so proficient that she couldn't imagine missing a putt. For several years, she had so much confidence that she never developed a fear that she would have a difficult second putt.

It's important to realize that you won't make most of the long putts. However, by practicing your short putts, you'll begin to gain the confidence to automatically make your *second* putt.

WHEN PUTTING, STROKE THROUGH THE BALL. KEEP YOUR PUTTER HEAD TRAVELING DIRECTLY TOWARD THE HOLE AND KEEP YOUR WRISTS FIRM.

Choosing a Putter

There are hundreds of putter styles, but they basically fall into two categories. "Blade" putters have a narrow head similar to a knife blade but somewhat thicker. "Mallet" head putters have a much thicker head.

On the professional tours you will see extra-long putters, putters of standard length, and everything in between. The immortal Bobby Jones used a very short putter. The professionals also use putters with heads that greatly vary. You need not copy a professional's putter just because you saw the pro make a few putts on television.

If you're a new golfer, ask your local professional to recommend a suitable putter. Most likely, he or she will let you experiment with the putter on the practice green. This way, you can eventually find the putter that feels right to you.

From time to time your stroke will break down. You do not need to change your putter. Just check your fundamentals. Is your grip correct? Is your stance in line to the hole? Are your eyes over the ball? Are you taking the putter blade straight back and straight through on the line to the hole? Does your left wrist remain frozen? Are you accelerating on your forward stroke?

With practice, you can become a very good putter just by sticking to these fundamentals.

4.

Short Shots

You've now mastered the basic putting stroke. Hopefully, you're becoming more accomplished with putting on the green and putting from the "fringe," the short grass around the green that is only slightly longer than the grass on the green. Let's move on to a more advanced shot.

For short shots between 10 and 150 yards, you'll use a variety of clubs. These clubs are longer than the conventional putter. You must now learn to put your feet and body in a different position when "standing up to the ball," or establishing your stance. This is the stance you will use for all of your clubs except your putter.

The swing we'll work on is a miniswing, but it's at the

root of the swings you'll make on almost every shot you'll hit—from any distance. Learning this swing will give you the basis of every swing, with the exception of difficult shots that will demand an expertise used only by the most advanced golfers. Later in this book, I'll help you learn how to hit these more difficult shots. Remember, at this point we are only considering the shot you must make under normal conditions.

The short shot will vary with the distance from the edge of the green to the "pin placement," or where the flagstick is located on the green. Sometimes you may need to carry the ball over a problem area, such as a water hazard or bunker that is situated between your ball and the green.

Unless you're facing an impossible shot, don't simply land the ball on the green. Always try to get the ball as close to the hole as possible. The closer you hit your ball to the hole, the fewer putts you'll have, and the lower your score will be.

On these short shots, including distances from which you would use irons ranging from the 5-iron to the wedge, your goal is consistency and accuracy.

As you begin to hit short shots, you should use your regular golf grip (explained in chapter 5). Take a relaxed stance with the ball in the middle of your stance. In other words, the ball should be an equal distance between your left foot and right foot.

One professional has a simple theory with which I agree. The theory is that swinging at the ball is like shaking hands. It's as simple as this: with your stance and body facing forward as you address the ball, imagine that you want to shake your left hand with someone standing immediately to your right. In a relaxed manner, you turn to your right and extend your left hand with your left palm perpendicular to the ground. Try this move without a club.

WHEN HITTING SHORT SHOTS, TAKE A RELAXED STANCE WITH THE BALL
IN THE MIDDLE OF YOUR STANCE AND YOUR HANDS SLIGHTLY AHEAD OF
THE BALL.

As you make your backswing, imagine that you want to shake left hands with someone standing to your right.

ON YOUR FOLLOW-THROUGH, IMAGINE THAT YOU WANT TO SHAKE
RIGHT HANDS WITH SOMEONE STANDING TO YOUR LEFT.

Your follow-through is much the same. Imagine that you want to shake right hands with someone standing to your left. Now, without using a club, turn naturally to your left and extend your right hand with your right palm perpendicular to the ground. The combination of these two moves is the basic swing you use for short shots.

With both hands on a club in a regular grip, try combining the two handshaking motions. Turn first to your right, then to your left. Be sure that your hands extend with the palms perpendicular to the ground.

You don't need to crouch or stiffen your body in a way that makes turning difficult. You want to extend your hand in a very natural way without leaning or swaying. This applies to both your left and right hands.

At the same time, you don't want to dip your head or raise it, nor do you want to elevate your shoulders. All you need to do is bring your left shoulder under your chin and extend your left hand to the imaginary person next to you.

Again, this applies to both the backswing and the follow-through. On your forward swing, your right shoulder stays under your chin to shake hands with the person to your left. Because this is a short swing, your feet should be fairly close together.

Naturally in shaking hands on both sides your shoulders and hips must turn freely, your knees must react, and, to a limited degree, your feet should react.

However, when shaking hands with your left hand to the right, your right knee must stay in position at all times and the left knee naturally move to the right. During this turn, the left knee should remain pointing at a spot behind the ball and should not move to the left.

The reverse is true when shaking hands with the right hand on the follow-through. The left knee should not sag but should remain in a comparative stance position.

After you have practiced these positions with a club, try hitting a few practice shots. Practice with your wedge, 9-iron, and 8-iron. If you can achieve these positions, you will have mastered some of the more important fundamentals of the golf swing.

You also need to know how far you can hit each of these clubs. After you've had a chance to practice using them, hit a few practice shots to gain a knowledge of how far you can hit each club. Hopefully, you have the opportunity to practice at a driving range or practice range with yardage markers. Hit four or five shots with your wedge first, then follow the procedure while using your 9-iron, 8-iron, and continue up to the 5-iron.

After hitting a solid shot and making a good follow-through, note how far the shot flies in the air and approximately how far it rolls once it lands. Repeat this with each club until you've learned approximately how far you hit each one—both how far the ball carries and how far it rolls.

5.

Getting a Grip on the Club

The grip is an important subject.

It is your only real physical contact with the golf club, and for many people it is difficult to learn. If you are a first-time golfer, I suggest you read this section as closely as possible with the understanding that you will need to return to it many times in your effort to improve your golf game. Golf is impossible without a proper grip. The grip—good or bad—has ramifications that can only be understood by advanced players. It's like the heart in the human body. Everything else can be okay, but, if it isn't right, the body cannot function properly.

Like chapter 3, this chapter is written for right-handed players, and left-handed golfers should simply mirror, or reverse,

WHEN GRIPPING THE CLUB WITH THE LEFT HAND, THE LAST THREE FINGERS ARE CLOSE TOGETHER AND HOLD THE CLUB SNUGLY.

the instructions. We'll begin by discussing the proper way to grip the club with the left hand. Be sure to study the photographs closely. They're your best guide to learning to grip the club properly. This is the most difficult subject for a student to understand, as well as for any author to explain.

New golfers should use the same grip for putting and for the full swing. Grip the club between one-half and one inch from the end of the grip. The grip of the club should fit in your left hand where the fingers join the palm. Your last three fingers are actually pressure points. They are closed snugly around the grip. The index finger curls naturally around the grip with the other three fingers.

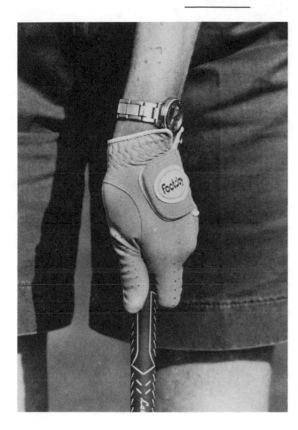

THE LEFT THUMB IS
PLACED DOWN THE
RIGHT SIDE OF THE
GRIP OF THE CLUB.

If the little finger of your left hand remains snug through-out the swing, the next two fingers will generally stay firm. This will help you swing correctly every time.

I once heard Bing Crosby elaborating on the grip. He said that you should hold the club firmly enough to squeeze toothpaste out of a tube very slowly. This is a great recommendation.

The proper angle of the shaft to your left hand is essential. The left thumb is placed down the right side of the grip. This means slightly to the right of the center of the grip of the club, not pointing straight down the shaft to the clubhead.

The grip of the club should lie diagonally from the base

IN THIS SIDE VIEW OF THE VARDON GRIP, YOU CAN SEE THE CORRECT POSITION OF THE FINGERS OF THE RIGHT HAND AND HOW THE LITTLE FINGER OF THE RIGHT HAND OVERLAPS THE FINGERS OF THE LEFT HAND.

of the index finger of your left hand and across the palm. If you hold your hands in a downward position, the end of this diagonal should be just below the pad located at the bottom of your hand opposite your left thumb.

Once you've put your left hand in position on the grip of the club, you'll notice a "v" made by the thumb and index finger. This v-shaped space should be closed, and the "v" should point to the center of the right shoulder.

Now for the grip with your right hand. With your left hand properly placed on the club, place your right hand on the grip. The grip of the club should lie in the channel formed in your right palm when your right fingers are bent. Your left thumb fits snugly under your right thumb.

WHEN YOUR RIGHT HAND IS ON THE CLUB, THE GRIP OF THE CLUB FITS SNUGLY IN THE CHANNEL FORMED BY YOUR BENT FINGERS.

As I mentioned in chapter 3, there are several grips: the baseball grip, the interlocking grip, and the Vardon, or overlapping, grip. All three grips work well and top professionals have succeeded with each.

The interlocking grip is usually used by golfers with small hands and short fingers; Jack Nicklaus uses this grip. The baseball grip is usually used by someone who simply likes the feel of it; Bob Rosburg uses this grip. It is also good if you're hindered by arthritic hands. The Vardon grip is preferred by most golfers. It helps you obtain additional distance and good hand action, giving you the preferred freedom of follow-through.

Everything I've told you to do so far can be applied to

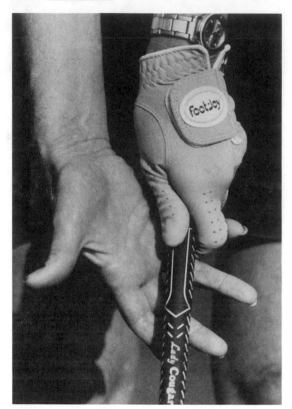

AFTER TAKING YOUR
GRIP WITH YOUR
LEFT HAND, WITH
THE "V" BETWEEN
THE LEFT THUMB
AND FOREFINGER
POINTING TO YOUR
RIGHT SHOULDER,
SIMPLY FOLD THE
FINGERS OF THE
RIGHT HAND OVER
THE GRIP. THE LITTLE
FINGER OF THE
RIGHT HAND CURLS
AROUND THE
KNUCKLE OF THE
LEFT FOREFINGER.

any of these three grips. But, as we continue, we are speaking only of the Vardon grip.

After placing your right thumb snugly over your left thumb, simply fold the little finger of your right hand over the index finger of your left hand. You could describe this movement as the curling of the right little finger around the exposed knuckle of the left index finger.

You have now formed a "v" between the thumb and index finger of your right hand. This "v" also points to your right shoulder. If it points beneath your right shoulder or above your right ear, the grip will be wrong.

The index finger of your right hand is wrapped firmly around the grip in the position for the swing. Your hands are

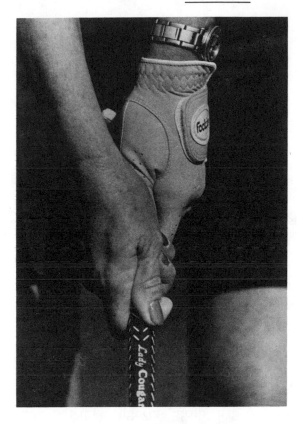

THE RIGHT AND LEFT HAND FIT TOGETHER SNUGLY. THE "V"S BETWEEN THE THUMBS AND FOREFINGERS SHOULD BE CLOSED.

completely together. They should feel almost melded in order to work together during the swing.

Some professionals claim that both hands should apply equal pressure on the grip of the club. I recommend that the pressure applied by your right hand be approximately one-half the pressure applied by your left hand. The reason I prefer this difference in pressure is that, during impact, your right hand must be the trigger for the long hit.

The right hand should be placed slightly to the right of the top of the shaft, or the part of the shaft facing skyward. Your right thumb and index finger should fit together as snugly as possible. This closes the "v" of your right hand. It's essential, because your right hand is vital for a flow of power.

Your left hand is the directional hand. Its influence is to guide the swing on the proper plane in the exact direction to strike the ball with the center of the clubface. At that point, your right hand must have the accelerated power to contact the ball as hard as possible while maintaining a smooth swing.

The information in this paragraph is for the advanced player. I suggest that the beginner ignore this part until the grip feels normal and is almost automatic. When some professionals want to "hook" a ball, or make the ball curve to the left, they will turn both hands more to the right side of the club with the clubface remaining in the same position as when they address the ball. When they want to "slice," or make the ball curve to the right, they turn their hands more left, and the "v"s point to the chin or even a little left of the chin. Personally, I use this method, but I believe the method described in the next paragraph is better for all but the most advanced players. Both methods take practice.

Instead of changing the position of your hands as described above, it's easier to grip more strongly with the right hand for a hook or more strongly with the left hand for a slice. This is less complicated and results in more consistent success.

Now that we've discussed the grip in some detail, I'll issue a warning. You must remember to keep the last three fingers of your left hand gripped firmly on the backswing—especially at the top of the backswing. Golfers frequently become careless about this point. It is a fault in my own swing. It feels good to loosen those three fingers, and I feel like I will get more clubhead speed if I do so. However, if you loosen those fingers you're inviting disaster. You'll have a tendency to hit with the body instead of with the hands. This is called "hitting from the top," and it can cause slicing, hooking, "topping the ball" (hitting it above its center), "hitting under the ball" (also called hit-

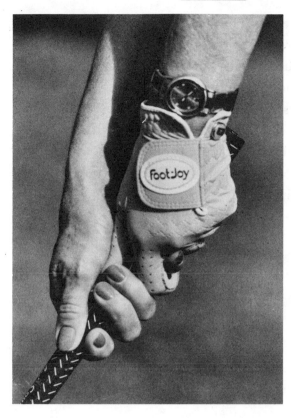

THIS IS AN INTER-
LOCKING GRIP. THE
LITTLE FINGER OF
THE RIGHT HAND IS
LOCKED BETWEEN
THE FIRST TWO
FINGERS OF THE LEFT
HAND INSTEAD OF
LYING ACROSS THE
KNUCKLE.

ting a "fat shot," which occurs when the clubhead strikes the ground before the ball), and a complete loss of control.

You've just read the fundamentals of the Vardon grip, in which the little finger of the right hand is placed over the knuckle of the left index finger. I believe the Vardon grip will help you have a smoother swing with more clubhead speed. As I've already mentioned, Jack Nicklaus, one of history's greatest golfers, uses an interlocking grip. The interlocking grip means that you lock your right little finger between your left index and middle fingers. They're actually intertwined. Examine the photographs closely.

Many people, especially people who are arthritic or have small hands, use either an interlocking grip or a baseball grip and find them to be more firm. However, I think both of these grips restrict a smooth flow to the ball and clubhead speed. No one can argue with the success of Nicklaus, but his grip is considered a bit unorthodox among top players.

The grips discussed in this chapter can be adapted, because every individual has different hands. Small or arthritic hands, for example, demand an adaptation. If other problems interfere with your grip, a good professional can help you establish a successful, repetitive grip.

6.

· ·

Addressing
the Ball

When you "address" the ball, you
establish your stance and ball position. Using a comfortable posture, stand in a normal way as if you were having a conversation
with someone, with the distance between your feet approximately equal to the width of your shoulders. For short shots,
your feet should be slightly closer together.

Bend slightly from the waist. Your rear end shouldn't settle
excessively but should stay slightly elevated and out. Jim Langley
is one professional who places much emphasis on this point.

You will constantly hear that you should "sit down" in
your stance. But sitting down restricts freedom of movement
and causes a sway or an up-and-down movement, which are
forbidden in golf.

THIS IS A NATURAL STANCE. THE DISTANCE BETWEEN THE INSIDES OF
THE FEET IS APPROXIMATELY EQUAL TO THE WIDTH OF THE SHOULDERS.

THE ARMS HANG NATURALLY WITH THE HANDS FAR ENOUGH FROM THE
BODY TO ALLOW ROOM TO MAKE A FREE SWING. NOTICE HOW THE LEFT
WRIST HANGS NATURALLY, NOT ARCHING UP OR DOWN.

Your left arm is neither hugging your body nor laying on your upper chest. Instead, it hangs freely as if you were walking. Your left arm can then swing without pressure.

When addressing the ball, or establishing your stance and ball position, your hands should hang comfortably, taking into account the length of the club. A general guideline is that there be four or five inches between your hands and your thighs. Your hands must not be overly extended, but your left hand must comfortably reach toward the ball without your wrist arching upward or pushing down so that it becomes an effort.

Your left arm is your guide dog; it directs the "line," or "plane." (The "line," or "plane," is an imaginary line from the beginning of the backswing all the way to the top of the backswing and forward to the completion of the follow-through.) The golf swing is an inside-to-outside motion on the downswing, so your right elbow should hang loosely and your left arm should be comfortably firm. Your right arm generates acceleration through the ball, powered by the right forearm and the hands.

It is simply a form, but one that is natural, easy, and proper.

Posture

For a drive or long shot, both shoulders must be aligned directly with your plane line, or where you want the ball to fly. (The plane will be explained in detail in chapter 7.) On a long shot, your left shoulder can be on line and your right shoulder slightly back.

The same is true for your hips and feet. The position of your feet, shoulders, and hips should be natural and in unison with your arms. They should squarely face the ball.

In golf, you often hear someone say after a bad shot, "I looked up." This isn't what really happened. Actually, they have

THIS IS VERY GOOD ALIGNMENT. THE SHOULDERS, HIPS, AND FEET ARE
ALIGNED ON PLANE.

reacted to a bad stance. The cause is usually due to bad posture. Bending over too much at address causes the player to make an upward swing. In other words, she's inadvertently correcting her lower posture. With the proper posture, your head will stay down.

Stance

The stance is basically the same for all full shots. As we progress, you will learn when to "open" your stance, which is done by moving your left foot back from a line perpendicular to the target line, and when to "close" your stance, which is done by pulling your right foot back from this perpendicular line.

The position of your feet is important for good balance. If you stand with your weight on your toes or your heels, you will drastically alter your shots because you'll lose your balance. Too much weight on your toes causes a slight lean forward, which will destroy your plane, cause you to hit the ball on the "heel" of the club, and reduce your distance. (The "heel" is the part of the clubface closest to the shaft; the "toe" is the part of the clubface farthest from the shaft.)

Too much weight on your heels will cause you to take the club back behind your plane. From there, you'll top the ball or mishit the shot.

Remember that your stance should be quite comfortable, with your weight evenly distributed as if you are standing in a normal, conversational position. This may sound complicated, but a good stance is easy to achieve. Don't underestimate its importance.

The weight distribution on your feet is also very important. On a drive or long shot, about sixty percent of your weight should be on your right foot. On shorter shots, sixty percent or

USING THE DRIVER AND FAIRWAY WOODS, THE BALL IS PLAYED EVEN
WITH THE LEFT HEEL. HEAD POSITION IS CRUCIAL. YOUR CHIN AND
EYES SHOULD BE POSITIONED SLIGHTLY BEHIND THE BALL.

more of your weight (depending on the distance) should be on your left foot at address.

On the shorter shots, you must contact the ball before the turf. On a good shot, you'll take a "divot" after hitting the ball. (A "divot" is a piece of turf removed from the ground by the impact of the clubhead.) You are hitting down on the ball. This will give you backspin and prevent a fat hit. Proper weight distribution, with more weight on our left side, will help you hit down on the ball.

Since you're seeking an aggressive swing, you'll need a good weight shift. A proper stance and proper weight distribution will also permit your legs to transfer your weight from the right side to the left side on the downswing.

Ball Position

Modern teaching often dictates that the ball remain in the same position relative to your left foot, or the same positon in your stance, for every shot. Others believe that the ball should be more in the middle of the stance for shorter shots. This will be your decision and executed in your own way. Whatever is most effective and comfortable is proper.

Head Position

Head postion needs to be stressed. On the drive, your chin and eyes should be positioned slightly behind the ball and even with your hands. For fairway woods and long shots, your eyes and chin should be in line with the ball. On all other shorter shots, the head is even with or slightly ahead of the ball.

7.

. . . .

The Plane

This is probably one of the most easily understood and definitely one of the most important subjects in learning the golf swing. As you already know, the plane is the imaginary line from the beginning of the backswing all the way to the top of the backswing and forward to the completion of the forward swing, or follow-through. It should be a common line for both the backswing and the forward swing, and it should never vary. Except when you are putting, you will have the same plane no matter which club you swing.

There are several critical points to the plane. They sound more complicated than they are. Ben Hogan describes the plane nicely in his book, *Five Lessons: The Modern Fundamentals of Golf.*

Hogan says to imagine a large sheet of glass. This sheet of glass has a hole in it for the golfer's head. If you put the bottom of the sheet at the golf ball and lean it over your shoulders with your head in the hole, it shows the plane of your swing.

Here's how I describe it. The plane of your swing is the path made by the club as you swing backward and forward. In making your backswing, the club shaft and clubhead must come between your ears and your shoulders. The same is true on the forward swing. The club must finish between your ears and your shoulders on the same line. This keeps the plane constant.

There are several ways to keep the plane constant. Do not pull your hands back with the clubhead following in what is called a "wristy" swing. The clubhead should be taken back firmly, but without tension, to position between your shoulders and ears, and your hands and wrists should flex a bit but never become flippy. You simply want to hit the ball solidly without having your wrists and hands totally frozen.

Your follow-through should be the same. A firm follow-through follows the plane on which you want to hit the ball.

As the distance of your shot increases, each phase of the backswing and the follow-through will increase. The plane will always stay the same. Nothing will stay frozen, but your body will remain firm. As the distance of your shots increase, your shoulder turn will also increase. On your backswing, your left shoulder moves under your chin; on your forward swing, your right shoulder moves under your chin.

Your hips turn away from the ball on your backswing and toward the ball, then past it, on your forward swing. Your left foot can either remain firmly on the ground or it may roll in toward your right foot. And, on the follow-through, your right foot may end up on its toe.

BE SURE TO STAY ON PLANE AFTER IMPACT WITH THE BALL.

Here's a good mental image. Upon impact, your body should be in the same postion as when you addressed the ball.

There is a statement made in golf that you must "clear" your left side. This is frequently misunderstood. You should simply and subtly permit your left side to "clear," or turn left, but you must first hit the ball with the left side and right side in the proper position. The left side clears only after you have hit the ball.

There are ways to obliterate a proper plane even before you begin to swing. Some golfers stand with their weight on their toes, taking the clubhead outside of the plane. Others, who put too much weight on their heels, draw their clubhead inside of the plane. But almost all good players do it correctly, taking the club back with their arms and hands and allowing their bodies to flow with the swing.

A modestly rigid left arm should be part of the "takeaway," or the first part of the backswing. To be natural, it would be like holding a bucket of paint with the left hand when taking your club away. Your arm must stay out, although it should be free and easy.

On the backswing, your right elbow stays close to your body. If it didn't, you could not permit your hands to rise to the horizontal line between your shoulder and ear. The swing should accelerate and be powerful enough that your arms release and follow through in their proper direction—your plane.

In the learning process, you must be careful to concentrate on not allowing the club shaft to go beyond a horizontal line at the top of the backswing. Going beyond that point can cause disaster.

One very delicate point is the precise point of impact. Most professionals who write about the swing discuss "clubhead speed," or the velocity of the clubhead at impact with the ball.

This is tremendously important, yet it's something of a fallacy. For example, one could attach a clubhead to a string, swing the clubhead around at super speeds, and then hit a golf ball with that speed. But there would be no *force* behind it, and the ball would travel only a short distance. There should be firmness in contact, and the timing of this firmness, as well as the release of the clubhead, is very precise. What I call a "flippy wrist" movement will not move the ball any appreciable distance.

All of these motions, which sound complicated but are simple if you try them as you swing a club, are designed to keep your swing on plane. In other words, your goal is to keep the club moving on the proper swing path. Once you can do this consistently, you are on your way to becoming a true golfer.

8.

·····································

Tempo, Timing, and Acceleration

You'll often hear the words "timing" and "tempo." Good timing happens when the individual components of the swing are connected—the downswing progresses with timed, accelerated power; the release takes place at the proper time; the plane is maintained; and the swing finishes with a proper follow-through.

Tempo is different from timing. Good tempo is achieved when you make a smooth transition from the backswing to the downswing. Many knowledgeable professionals teach golfers to pause at the top of the backswing to mentally prepare for the downswing. So many golfers use this pause effectively that it's difficult to disagree.

Tempo prepares you for the speed and power of the down-swing. Most golfers don't pause, nor do they need to. A slow backswing with a smooth transfer of power to the downswing is a key to having great tempo, which is of maximum importance. The choice of whether or not to pause is yours.

Through impact, you are not simply hitting the ball but lashing through the ball on plane. You're releasing with maxi-mum and firm hand power, whether you feel as if you're hitting through the ball or swinging through the ball. This lashing of the ball is common to both types of swings and results in distance.

The muscles, size, and weight of a player don't deter-mine distance. Coordination, timing, proper shoulder and body movement, and release are the deciding factors of distance.

I foresee the day when a woman will destroy the fallacy that men hit the ball farther than women.

"Acceleration," or the increasing speed of the downswing, is the key to distance and the resulting good scores. You cannot reach higher goals in golf without acceleration.

In chapter 3, you read that a good golfer accelerates even when stroking a putt. Well, the longer the shot, the more accel-eration is necessary.

In discussing acceleration, I am speaking only of the downswing, or hitting through the ball. Some professionals have gone so far as to claim that the backswing has no importance compared to the accelerated downswing. However, I believe that a good backswing is crucial. In a backswing, you place the club shaft, the clubhead, the arms, and the rest of the body in position to hit through the ball with maximum acceleration. Golfers can't afford to overaccelerate, but, for maximum power, controlled acceleration must exist.

A good backswing places your feet, knees, hands, shoul-ders, and arms in position. It's what I describe as a loading process.

One of the easiest ways to understand this procedure is to watch a baseball player swing a bat. The player will get the bat in position to swing at the ball. Baseball players have no backswing procedure as such. Some have idiosyncrasies, such as tapping home plate with the end of the bat. Many even place their bat in an improper position until just before the pitch. Others wave the bat before the pitch is thrown. They may even swing on an improper plane or waste acceleration with a chopping motion.

After the ball is thrown, however, most baseball players swing as fast as possible. The bat's speed accelerates through the moment when the bat makes contact with the ball. Baseball has other similarities to golf. Like a fine golfer, the pitcher is slow in his windup and then throws in a hard, accelerating motion.

Many athletes in other sports, such as volleyball (when spiking) and tennis, use acceleration. Only a few use a loading process. This may be the reason many women who play softball become long hitters as golfers—because they are adept and natural at acceleration.

All levels of golfers, from beginners to the most advanced players, can improve acceleration and, therefore, improve their games.

Most golf club manufacturers seek to develop a club shaft, and even clubheads, to increase controlled acceleration without creating problems, such as excessive "torque." ("Torque" is the twist of a club shaft.)

Shafts, originally made of wood, have been made of steel, stainless steel, graphite, aluminum, boron, and a combination of materials. Each development is an attempt to increase acceleration with increased clubhead speed. If a club is constructed of a material that can release at the greatest possible acceleration and still have the stiffest possible shaft, it almost guarantees great distance. Similar to manufacturers, good teachers are striving to teach their students to accelerate by developing a good golf swing.

9.

The Components of a Good Swing

You've just learned that good timing occurs when the individual components of the swing are connected. In this chapter, we'll look at each component in detail. When you are able to make each part of the swing correctly and connect them with good timing, you'll be ready to hit full golf shots.

The Take-away

The "take-away," or the first part of the backswing, is a loading process. It prepares you for acceleration through the ball on the downswing. Improper position on the backswing makes a proper downswing almost impossible.

The take-away is a continuation of the posture and stance. Remember to stay firm and keep your left arm comfortably straight. On a drive, keep your left arm extended as long as possible, stay relaxed, and prepare for your acceleration down through the ball. Don't become so tense that you grit your teeth or stiffen your muscles.

The clubhead should be taken back on plane. Unless you become tense, the rest of your body will follow. Be sure to keep your right knee and leg in place. Your hips and shoulders should turn away, and your left knee should move behind the ball, pointing down and somewhat toward your right knee.

I want to emphasize your hands. They should not fan out or open, but they should open naturally as your backswing continues. Your hands open as a natural result of the turning of your shoulders and body in the handshaking motion. You should not block them or attempt to keep the clubface square. This would prevent your hands from moving correctly to the top of the swing. At the top, the clubface should be vertical—not pointing to the sky or facing the ground to any degree.

The Backswing

If you watch other golfers, you see many make the backswing as fast as they make the downswing. Even a few professionals do this. They claim that this is their tempo, but few if any have ever been successful with this swing.

Try to have the club shaft horizontal at the top of the backswing. If you go past horizontal, you're generally letting go of the grip with the last three fingers of your left hand.

The backswing uses the entire right side of your body—it's not an arm-only swing. A natural turn-away from the ball

REMEMBER THE HANDSHAKING POSITION ON THE TAKE-AWAY. YOUR
LEFT ARM SHOULD REMAIN COMFORTABLY EXTENDED. YOUR HANDS
HAVE NOT FANNED OPEN, AND THE LEFT WRIST REMAINS IN A STRAIGHT
LINE.

IF THE CLUB SHAFT GOES *PAST* HORIZONTAL AT THE TOP OF THE
BACKSWING, IT'S A BIT MORE DIFFICULT TO CONTROL THE CLUB AND
THE SHOT.

THIS IS A FULLY LOADED POSITION.

BE SURE THAT YOUR THUMBS ARE UNDER THE CLUB SHAFT AT THE TOP OF THE BACKSWING. THIS WILL HELP YOU MORE FIRMLY CONTROL THE CLUB.

with your left arm and hand helps control the plane and puts you in a fully loaded position. Please note that I have not mentioned your left shoulder. Your shoulder turn begins as a result of the take-away. A turn-away with your left arm and hand prepares for acceleration through the ball.

At the top of the backswing both thumbs must be underneath the club shaft. In the take-away, your left hand and arm are not pushed back by the body at any time. It's a free movement that the rest of the body will follow.

One point deserves special consideration—the line of your left hand and the club shaft to the line of the plane. If your left hand and the shaft are pointed either outside or inside of the plane line, your shot is ruined.

If the direction of your left hand and the club shaft point out and away from the plane, you're either swinging too flat or allowing the clubface to open excessively. Conversely, if your left hand and the shaft are pointed inside the plane, you're taking the club up too steeply, which results in the club being in a hook position. Your left hand and the club shaft must always point to the plane line.

Remember, on the take-away your body must never rise or sway, especially at the top of the backswing. Your hips will turn away as much as forty-five degrees, and your right knee will remain in address position. The stability of your right knee is a point of resistance to gain leverage and lag and to enact full power. Your right knee stabilizes your swing. In practice, you can gain this objective by placing a ball under your right foot toward the outside and just below the toes. (You're actually standing on the ball with your foot tilted inward.) This will keep your right leg and knee in position.

Your left knee should point slightly down and behind the ball at the top of the backswing. However, your left foot

ON THE BACKSWING THE HIPS TURN AS MUCH AS FORTY-FIVE DEGREES
AWAY FROM THE BALL, BUT THE RIGHT KNEE POINTS DOWN AND
SLIGHTLY BEHIND THE BALL.

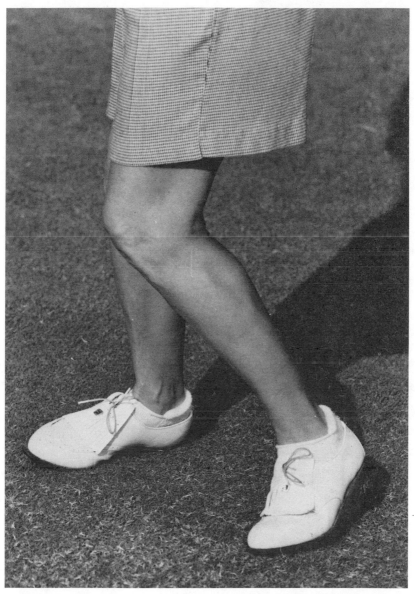

THE LEFT HEEL IS SLIGHTLY ELEVATED AT THE TOP OF THE BACKSWING.

AT THE TOP OF THE BACKSWING, YOUR RIGHT HAND SHOULD BE ABLE
TO HOLD A TRAY OF GLASSES. THIS MEANS THAT THE RIGHT ELBOW IS
CLOSE TO THE BODY AND POINTS TO THE GROUND AND THE LEFT WRIST
IS IN A STRAIGHT LINE.

should never rest on its toes. Instead, it should roll slightly to the right—but only slightly.

One very important point to know about the swing is that "pulling the trigger," or starting the downswing, begins with your left heel. Your left heel must return to its address position. It should not settle to the left or right of the address position. For this reason, your left toes never move after address. Remember, your left foot rolls slightly.

Watch the professionals on television. At the top of their backswings, their shoulders are fully wound. The shoulders actually form a "T" to the plane line.

Remember that the body does not bend, either to the left or the right, on the backswing. Such a bend generally results in disaster.

The position of the left hand and wrist at the top of the backswing is a subject of debate among professionals. My personal feeling is that the arm, wrist, and hand form a straight line. The wrists are neither bent up nor down but must stay in a constant line with the hands and arms.

At the top of the backswing, your right hand should be able to hold a tray of glasses without the glasses dropping or their contents spilling. This is an example of why you should not cup or dip your left wrist. Your right elbow must point down toward the ground and be near the side of your body.

The Downswing

Now that you've worked on the take-away and the backswing, you're ready to begin work on the downswing. Your goals are acceleration, consistency, and accuracy. To achieve this, the clubhead and the plane must stay in position. If your body moves correctly, all of your preparations on the backswing will yield in your favor. Stay with your plane, don't second guess, and you'll hit the ball properly with acceleration.

On the downswing, we'll first learn to pull the trigger. You do this by re-establishing your left heel in its address position. On the backswing you learned to roll your left foot to the right, allowing the heel to lift slightly. We begin the downswing by planting the left heel in its original position. Not to the right or left of its original position, but as close as possible to where it was at address. This motion allows the left side of your body to lead the downswing. When the left side leads, the hand action is slightly delayed, giving you more acceleration, more distance, and an overall better shot.

Next, pull the heel of your left hand to the plane and concentrate on the ball. Remember, the clubhead lags and remains behind the hands until it's time for a forceful release, which allows the clubhead to accelerate through the ball.

When you make contact with the ball, your shoulders must be square to the plane. When you begin the hit, you begin with your left foot, your arms, and a delayed unbreaking of your wrists. If you begin by pulling your shoulders or turning your hips to the left, your swing will be out of sync. Instead, your hips slide laterally in a slightly sideways motion. They only turn left after impact with the ball.

Here's another important point. Your left wrist breaks at impact and not before. I call this the "belt buckle" application. The heel of your hand must not pass your belt buckle until impact. If the heel of the hand remains ahead of the clubface at impact, a sliced or "pushed" shot will result. (A "pushed" shot is different from a slice, because it starts to the right and continues to the right in a straight line.) Also, your left wrist should not

AS THE FORWARD SWING BEGINS, THE LEFT HEEL RETURNS TO ITS
ADDRESS POSITION ON THE TURF.

ON THE DOWNSWING PULL THE HEEL OF THE LEFT HAND TOWARD THE PLANE. CONCENTRATE ON THE BALL.

MAINTAIN YOUR INSIDE-TO-OUTSIDE SWING BY MAKING SURE THAT
YOUR RIGHT ARM AND ELBOW REMAIN UNDERNEATH YOUR LEFT ARM.

break before passing the buckle. If the heel of your left hand stops and your right hand crosses the left before striking the ball, you will have equally poor results. The ball will go left or stay on the ground.

Your shoulders are an important factor and permit you to use your legs. They also permit your right elbow to remain beneath your left arm, which is extremely important. You need the power of your right hand upon impact. You cannot maintain a modest inside-to-outside swing without your right arm remaining underneath your left arm through impact.

Making Contact

Keep the body steady and release the clubhead by hitting the ball as hard as possible with your right hand providing most of the power. Stay on plane and keep a firm grip with the last three fingers of your left hand. Be sure that you don't try to increase swing speed by prematurely turning your left shoulder or left hip. Remember, your hips first move laterally and then turn *after* impact with the ball.

The lash of the swing must be so pronounced that you cannot avoid following through. But a word of warning—the player who cannot wait to hit the ball usually self-destructs when swinging down. She hurries at the top and cannot wait for the proper time to release. As a result, the release comes too early.

After placing your left heel in position, your left arm and your hands begin to swing down before the shoulders. This prevents the mass of the body from trying to aid the swing. Concentrate on keeping your right elbow beneath your left arm. The club shaft must remain behind your hands as long as possible.

THE HIPS SLIDE LATERALLY AT THE START OF THE DOWNSWING AND ONLY TURN LEFT AFTER THE BALL IS HIT.

Also, a good hint to remember is that the arms and hands remain below the chin during the entire swing. Releasing early results in a loss of power and clubhead speed. To be a superior golfer, release at the proper time determines acceleration, clubhead speed, and firmness, all of which result in distance. Swinging too fast also destroys the ability to release at the proper time and to move all of the swing components together in proper sequence.

The Follow-through

After impact, your left arm continues down the plane with the same speed. Your left hip is now turning to the left (after sliding laterally). This is called "clearing the left hip"; it permits the follow-through.

As previously stated, the entire swing must be so forceful that you cannot prevent a follow-through. To finish properly, the clubhead should go around your shoulders, finish in a vertical position, or touch the buttocks. A vertical follow-through indicates that the balance and address position were incorrect. Either your body was too erect during the address, or you did not bend properly from the waist. Your right leg, especially your right knee, must move left with the downswing, and the hips must move laterally through impact.

On completion of the swing your body is balanced, your chest faces the target (plane line), your hands are at left-ear level, and both elbows are pointing toward the ground. All of this results from your belt buckle facing the target and a firm left leg. Your right knee should be close to your left and your right foot should have rolled slightly on its toes by the force of the swing through the ball.

AFTER IMPACT, THE LEFT ARM CONTINUES DOWN THE PLANE. THE LEFT HIP HAS NOW CLEARED.

FOR A GOOD, FULL FINISH OF THE SWING, YOUR WEIGHT IS ON YOUR
LEFT SIDE, YOUR BELT BUCKLE FACES THE HOLE, YOUR LEFT LEG IS FIRM,
YOUR RIGHT FOOT HAS ROLLED ON ITS TOE, YOUR ELBOWS ARE POINT-
ING TOWARD THE GROUND, AND YOUR HANDS ARE EVEN WITH YOUR
LEFT EAR.

Reviewing the Full Swing

It is helpful to practice with only your left arm and hand swinging the club. Swing down through the ball. It is important that the last three fingers of your left hand remain firm but not in a stranglehold.

Your right shoulder stays inside and does not move forward, but this is natural and certainly simple. Your shoulders will be more in line with the plane (with no conscious effort). Upon impact, they should not pull or turn left to help speed the swing but should be square with the line of the plane.

As the heel of your left foot returns to address position and your left arm and both hands move down, your shoulders should feel passive. Your hips should slide laterally, not turn left, until the clubhead meets the ball. You must continue the power of the impact down the plane and keep your shoulders and hips square to the ball as long as possible.

The moment the downswing begins, a long hitter has achieved a full shoulder turn and her hands have gone as high as possible without passing the horizontal line. The shaft remains parallel to the ground at the top of the swing. This is a key to distance and acceleration.

A few players are able to take a shorter swing or a three-quarter swing and still obtain maximum distance (e.g., senior professional Doug Sanders), but they have exceptionally strong forearms and hands.

10.

....

Beware of Hazards

Hitting from the rough and wet grass arc similar shots. In some respects, they are similar to sand shots. That's why I have combined the three different shots in this chapter with a concentration on bunker shots.

The Rough

Many courses today have thick, tall grass around the greens. Although I don't like this type of design and the resulting difficult maintenance, it's quickly becoming a part of modern golf. The people who are responsible for this very high fringe and rough obviously have a distorted sense of humor.

Actually, the Rules of Golf, which are approved by the United States Golf Association (USGA) and the Royal and Ancient Golf Club of St. Andrews, Scotland, do not recognize or acknowledge the word "rough." Again, distorted thinking. The Rules of Golf simply state that the term "through the green" excludes tees and greens; it does not mention the fairway and the rough. These ruling powers of golf, however, do frequently describe the "closely mown area," thereby acknowledging there is an area that is not closely mown, or a rough. Still, they never admit it.

I have no idea why such complicated language exists in the Rules of Golf. Many unnecessarily wordy phrases in the Rules could be eliminated by simply using the word "rough."

Why do I stress that it's ridiculous not to recognize the word "rough"? I do so because every single golfer acknowledges the word, uses it, and refers to it frequently. So, in this book, I am going to discuss the rough.

The long grass, or rough, not closely mown around the green poses special problems. There are different types of grass, such as Bermuda, bent grass, bluegrass, and various hybrids. Each type of grass plays differently. Rather than individually discussing the play from each type of grass and the character of each one, I think it is better for you to adjust to each when you are playing the course. This way you will learn from experience. The primary goal in hitting the ball out of long grass is to hit it solidly. The ball may be sitting up on top of the grass, or it may be nestled in high grass.

If it is sitting on top of the grass, you must be very careful not to hit underneath the ball. If it is nestled in high grass, however, the technique for hitting the ball will be vastly different.

If the ball is nestled, you must judge how hard to hit it. Many great golfers use the same "explosion shot" they use from

IF YOUR BALL IS NEAR THE GREEN BUT NESTLED IN HIGH GRASS, TRY AN EXPLOSION SHOT. USING YOUR SAND WEDGE, AIM YOUR STANCE TO THE LEFT OF THE HOLE, OPEN THE CLUBFACE SO THAT IT FACES THE HOLE, AND MAKE A NICE SLOW SWING AS YOU WOULD IN A BUNKER.

the sand. Here's how to make this shot: using your pitching wedge, address the ball as you would in a bunker, with an open stance and the clubface aiming directly at the hole; take the club back slightly outside, quickly cocking your wrists; with a nice slow swing, hit slightly behind the ball; and be sure to follow through.

Another common technique is to play the shot as you would a normal pitch shot but "close" the clubface slightly and expect the ball to pop up and run some distance. A third way to play this shot is to "open" the clubface and simply try to contact the ball solidly, again, expecting the ball to run more than ususal. (To close the clubface means to turn it to the left, and to open the clubface means to turn it to the right.) All of these techniques can be successful, so choose the one most comfortable for you.

The ball will run on these shots because there is grass between the clubface and the ball on contact. It is the grass that prevents your ball from having much "backspin," the spin that makes the ball stop quickly.

Landing the ball close to the hole from high grass requires practice and experience. Grass types also have an effect on how cleanly you are able to strike the ball, and only experience can help you learn how hard to swing. Soft grass, such as bent grass, is somewhat easier to swing through. Whereas wiry grasses, such as Bermuda, give more resistance and demand a firmer stroke.

If the ball is just a few inches from the green in long grass, you may want to experiment with using a sand wedge. Instead of using your usual technique for a bunker shot, simply try to contact the "equator," or the middle, of the ball with the bottom edge of the clubface. Strike the ball with about the same speed as you would a putt of the same distance. This shot takes a tremendous amount of practice and very good nerves, but it's an excellent shot to learn if you frequently play a course that has high grass, or rough, around the greens.

Long shots from the rough can be difficult. The first rule is to get out. To do so, you must first judge the texture, length, and thickness of the grass. This will help you decide how hard to swing and which club to use.

In light rough, a sweeping swing can be successful. Open the clubface slightly, aim directly at your target, and make a smooth, sweeping swing. But, if the grass is wiry, long, and thick, a sweeping swing won't do the job.

IF YOUR BALL IS JUST A FEW INCHES FROM THE GREEN IN HIGH GRASS, YOU MIGHT WANT TO TRY THIS SHOT. USING YOUR WEDGE OR SAND WEDGE, STRIKE THE BALL AT ITS EQUATOR. HIT THE BALL AS FIRMLY AS YOU WOULD STROKE A PUTT FROM THE SAME DISTANCE.

In moderately long rough, women almost always have more success using a 5-, 6-, or 7-wood. These clubs are easier to use for longer shots than long irons. If the grass is thick and moderately deep, swing one club more than you would from the same distance in the fairway. (Using one club more means using a club one number lower than you normally would for that distance.) Open the clubface slightly, use a more erect swing, and take the club up quickly on the backswing, hitting the ball with a descending blow. This will help you make better contact with the ball. Try to swing on a bit of an outside-to-inside plane. Allow for a slice, which means you should aim slightly to the left of your target.

THE 7-WOOD IS
OFTEN USEFUL FOR A
SHOT OUT OF HEAVY
ROUGH.

Wet Grass

When playing on wet grass on the fairway, you should be sure to contact the ball first. The clubhead will not bounce into the ball, as it would on a dry fairway, if you hit slightly behind it. Instead, the wet grass will cling to the clubhead. The dimples of the ball will also be filled with water, and the ball won't fly as high as it normally would. Take this lower flight into consideration; it may cause you to decide to use a higher lofted club. If the grass is wet, your ball won't roll much, so you'll have to depend on carry to get the ball to your target. In these conditions, the clubhead must contact the ball cleanly.

Of course, there's always an exception. Whether in the fairway or in the rough, if the ball is sitting well on top of the grass, it is actually feasible to hit a driver. Because of the elevated position of the ball, it will become airborne and the result will be a good long shot.

Often when your ball lands adjacent to a bunker or water hazard near the green, the grass is thick and heavy. Use your trusty sand wedge, especially if the ball must land softly and roll very little. With a little practice, you can learn to open the clubface slightly so that the ball will fly at a higher trajectory and have less roll. It's a fun shot, but you must be firm and stay on plane. At impact, make sure the clubhead goes through the shot, but don't allow your right hand to cross over your left on the follow-through.

Every once in a while, for fun and practice, place a ball on top of the grass. Open the face of your sand wedge as much as possible. Take a big, full swing. The ball will fly straight up and travel only ten to twenty yards. It's fun, and, while the need for such a shot is rare, there is an occasional instance calling for this approach.

Bunkers

On occasion your ball will end up in a bunker, commonly called a sand trap. It's semantics, but to be absolutely *legal* this part of the chapter is subtitled "bunkers."

A ball in a bunker is calamity for the beginning golfer, but experience and practice make bunker shots challenging and fun. Gary Player, among men professionals, and Kathy Whitworth, among women professionals, are far superior to their peers in hitting out of sand. Jack Nicklaus, on the other hand, lacks proficiency out of sand. Some observers claim that in his prime Jack was rarely in the sand and, therefore, is comparatively inexperienced.

My early years as a golfer were spent on courses that had no bunkers. A bunker is very expensive to maintain and requires a special type of sand. When my wife was first learning to play golf, we went to Spain with twenty-two very accomplished golfers for a golf holiday. On the second hole, my wife hit her ball into the sand. She took six shots and suffered considerable embarrassment trying to get out of that despicable place. I'm happy to say that today she is a very fine player and a little more experienced in playing from sand, so bunkers are no longer a problem.

On another occasion, I recall a friend from Iowa, Dr. Collison, landing in a bunker for the first time ever. He had a perfect lie, within eighteen inches of the green. White-faced in rage, he sputtered, "How the #*@# do you get out of this?"

Although it wasn't within the Rules, I took pity on him and drew a line one and a half inches behind the ball, telling him that the line was where the club must contact the sand and that he must follow through after hitting underneath the ball. Dr. Collison did not own a sand wedge. Using his pitching wedge and being cautious that the wedge didn't dig too deeply, he was amazed when the ball reacted better than if he had putted it from the same distance. He was stunned. Normally he was a generous man, but, despite his success, he was still so angry that he wouldn't even buy me a drink. At that time, his temper was so great that he broke several pipe stems during a round of golf; perhaps he felt that that expense was enough.

There are many types of sand wedges, all with different angles between the clubface and the shaft. The "flange," which is the slightly rounded bottom of the sand wedge, can vary from a modest width to an extreme width. If you are a beginning golfer, use a standard sand wedge with a nice wide flange. You can make comparisons by looking at an assortment of sand wedges. Very wide-flanged or narrow-flanged sand wedges are specialized clubs that should be considered only by the most advance golfers.

To become an expert at hitting out of the sand, you must practice a variety of shots. The types of shots are as limitless as your imagination. Here are just a few varieties: a normal lie, a buried lie, a "fried egg" lie (a lie where the ball is half-buried in the sand), a lie near the lip of the bunker, a ball buried deep in a footprint, or a high elevation in front of the ball. Variety makes bunker play a game in itself.

You will have wet sand, coarse sand, firm sand, and fluffy sand. This part of the game challenges your imagination, and you'll find that the best way to deal with a sand shot is by making up a shot or learning from experience. In bunkers, always be sure to keep your hands inside the plane when making your shot and follow-through.

If your ball is buried in a deep footprint, it is almost impossible to get out. Instead of suffering through many futile attempts, simply take a penalty stroke under the "unplayable lie" rule and drop your ball within the bunker. You'll no doubt get a much better lie. Of course, the first thing you should learn is how to get the ball out of the sand. Then you can worry about how to get it close to the hole.

The Basic Bunker Shot

In a bunker, especially a greenside bunker, your stance must be firm. To achieve a firm stance, wiggle your feet until they are firmly planted in the sand. This allows you to have limited, but firm, foot action. This stance is always slightly open, and the clubhead should be slightly open. This means your ball will fly somewhat to the right of the line of your stance. Grip down a bit on the club, about two inches from the end of the grip. With your feet planted you are closer to the ball, so you must shorten your grip on the club. This shot does not demand power, although you must first swing firmly. It is a finesse shot.

The distance the ball must carry depends on how far you are from the flagstick. In some cases, you may also have to hit the shot quite high in order to carry, or get over, the lip of the bunker. There will be times when that elevation is so steep that you have to forget trying to hit the green and simply hit the ball out of the bunker. On such shots, you may have to hit the ball sideways or even backwards.

The variety that exists in bunker shots is illustrated by a shot my daughter faced when playing in a major tournament in the Midwest. With a somewhat shaky lead in the tournament, she landed in one of the few greenside bunkers. The sand was wet, the bunker had no lip, and she had a good lie, so she chose to putt it, stroking the ball to within inches of the hole. It was that simple.

For the sand shot that is not extremely long and has a good lie, a good way to judge distance is to imagine that you are throwing the ball toward the hole underhanded. The force with which you would throw the ball is the same force you should use when swinging your sand wedge.

When your ball lands in a bunker, try to assess your shot while standing outside the bunker. Determine the distance the ball must be hit, then imagine making a suitable swing for that distance while making a practice swing standing outside the bunker. Remember, you cannot take practice swings in a bunker or a hazard. It helps to take your practice swing by slightly contacting the turf.

YOUR FEET SHOULD BE SOMEWHAT DUG INTO THE SAND FOR A SHOT FROM THE BUNKER. THIS WILL GIVE YOU A FIRM STANCE.

In your practice swing, be careful not to allow your right hand to cross over your left or to let the clubface pass your left hand. You may want to keep your left hand in position on the club, enter the bunker, and swing just as easily, or as forcefully, as if you're throwing the ball to the hole.

In hitting the typical shot, your sand wedge should contact the sand approximately one and a half inches behind the ball. Simply try to slip the club under the ball by hitting the sand. Remember to keep your right elbow in, limit your body movement, and stay on plane.

If your ball is in a fried-egg lie, you'll need to close your clubface so that the sand wedge can more easily cut through the sand instead of bouncing off the sand. Practice will help you learn how much to close the clubface. Hit several inches behind the ball and try to follow through. The ball will probably run more, but it will generally become elevated enough to clear the bunker lip. This is because the force of the sand squares the clubface.

Don't think about carrying the ball to the hole in the air, because this shot will run. Hit it delicately, but follow through.

If your shot is extremely long, don't permit your right hand to cross over your left hand. However, if you need to hit a long sand shot, the swing will be much like that of a wedge shot and your follow-through will be normal—just follow through as you would on any full shot.

At times, you may use a pitching wedge, especially in wet sand. The ball will run more, but the narrow flange will more easily cut through the sand. When using a pitching wedge, be sure not to hit the ball with such a descending blow that the wedge buries itself in the sand and prevents your follow-through. Since it has a tendency to cut too deeply, be cautious. The bounce of the "sole," or the bottom of the club, of a regular

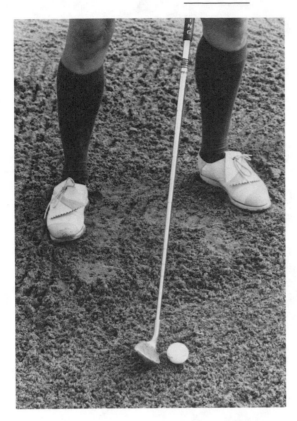

FOR A BUNKER SHOT THAT DOESN'T NEED TO TRAVEL TOO FAR AND HAS A GOOD LIE, YOUR CLUB SHOULD STRIKE THE SAND ABOUT 1½ INCHES BEHIND THE BALL.

wedge is less than that of the sand wedge. You can play with the same stance, swing with the same force, but the ball will not stop as quickly. When using a pitching wedge, you can try the same trick as with your sand wedge: calculate your distance as if you threw the ball on the green and let it roll to the hole.

Fairway Bunkers

The long sand shot is typically from fairway bunkers fifty or more yards from the green. If your ball is buried, just try to hit it out. Such an unlucky break is what golfers call the "rub of

IF THE BUNKER SHOT IS NOT EXTREMELY LONG, YOUR RIGHT HAND
SHOULD NOT CROSS OVER YOUR LEFT ON YOUR FOLLOW-THROUGH.

the green." Smile and swear to yourself, but remember that it sometimes happens to all of us.

Normally, a ball doesn't easily bury in a fairway bunker. It usually lies cleanly on the sand. To hit this shot, hit one club more than you normally would at this distance. Limit your body action, try to swing mostly with your shoulders and arms, and hit the shot cleanly, striking the ball before the sand. Never hit the sand first. And, since it's difficult to hit a really good shot from a fairway bunker, always play it safe by making sure you're not trying to carry a lake, pond, or similar hazard.

You must also grip down on the club, which is why you use a stronger club for the shot. Contact the ball first and don't try to overpower the shot. I agree with the theory that, on a long bunker shot, it is better to hit the ball a little "thin," or a little above the ball's center, than a little fat. If you contact the sand first, your shot will yield very little distance. If you hit it a little thin, you can often gain a lot of run, or roll, and your shot will come closer to landing where you want it.

When my son and daughter were playing the Kings course at Gleneagles Golf Club in Scotland, my son hit a ball into a fairway bunker on the eighteenth hole. The face of the bunker was so high that it wasn't feasible to attempt hitting the ball on the green. The smart shot was to simply play a shot to the side or even to hit the shot backwards. Because he had an excellent score at this point, he elected to go for the green. He hit a full shot toward the green, the ball glanced off the bunker's front lip, and it landed exactly where it started. He was livid until he saw us rolling with laughter and realized how funny it was.

If your shot is really impossible—sorry, again it's simply the rub if the green—take a one stroke penalty under the unplayable lie Rule and drop the ball within two club lengths of

ON A SHOT FROM A FAIRWAY BUNKER, BE SURE TO HIT THE BALL BEFORE THE SAND.

your bad lie. You must drop it in the bunker and no nearer the hole.

If your ball is on a downhill lie, you must use a more lofted club and face the consequences. Don't try a shot you are incapable of making, just get out.

May you become skilled at hitting out of the sand but never need to!

11.

. . . .

Common Problems
and Their Cures

It is very popular in golf books to
advocate positive thinking. Sports psychologists stress that you
must never emphasize what is wrong but stress the positive and
all of your problems on the course will disappear. Sounds great!

Unfortunately, positive thinking does not cure the temporary problems in a swing. Almost all professionals have at least
one or two "swing thoughts" to correct problems that occur in
the middle of a round. This allows them to at least salvage the
round if not score very well. Swing thoughts are the key to
correcting problems on the course.

After addressing the ball, it is difficult to make more than
one or two corrections in the swing. Most golfers, however, try

to analyze why they are doing something wrong and correct it. Therefore, this chapter considers the most common problems and how to solve them.

Golf's teaching professionals are here to help us. Sometimes they teach us to play golf, but more often they help us solve a temporary problem in our game.

Both the instructor and the golfer first have to decide what the problem is. Often, golfers will simply use a "Band-Aid," or a temporary solution to a problem, and work on its origin later. An example of a Band-Aid is a golfer who slices frequently aiming to the left of the target to compensate for the slice.

You may not experience every problem addressed in this chapter. However, it's good for reference, self-analysis, and helping your successful search for the solution. You will conduct your search at the practice range. You must carefully test yourself and, if needed, employ your professional to assist you. Your professional can immediately assess your problem and, if he or she is proficient, discover its basic cause.

Golf problems often demand much analysis, so explanations and corrections vary in length. The necessary changes may be few or many. The solutions may be brief, or they may require much attention and work.

Some people, like Ben Hogan, are perfectionists. In one tournament, Hogan was "fading" the ball, or making it travel in a slight left-to-right pattern, more than he wanted. A fellow professional suggested an adjustment, but Hogan explained that he never corrects his game while playing. He did it in practice, and sometimes a minute change in his swing would take six or seven months to perfect. Most golfers try to make a correction in a much shorter time, even in the middle of a round. Few of us demand that the change is permanent, automatic, and ingrained in our muscle memory.

Use this chapter as a reference and return to it as often as needed. When a section relates to your problem, study it. If you think you know what you are doing wrong, go to the practice range, apply the cures, and see if it solves the problem.

Slicing

Unfortunately, when you slice your shot suffers in two different ways. You suffer both loss of distance and loss of accuracy. These losses are much too great to tolerate. We slice simply because the clubhead crosses the ball from right to left upon impact, with the face either square or open. This causes the ball to spin left to right. To find out why you are slicing, ask yourself the following questions.

1. Are you swinging on plane, or does the clubhead impact the ball from the outside to the inside of the plane?
2. Are the last three fingers of your left hand gripped firmly throughout the swing?
3. Is your right elbow staying near your body on the downswing?
4. On your forward swing, does your right shoulder spin left, or does it go out, instead of under, your chin?
5. Has your left heel returned squarely to the address position, or did it move to the right of that position?
6. Are the "v"s of your grip pointing to your right shoulder?
7. Upon impact, your shoulders, knees, head,

and hips must be square to the line of the
target. Are they only even with the ball
after you turn left?

8. Has the heel of your left hand passed the
belt buckle before impact? It should not.
It must return to address position at impact.

9. Has the ball been hit with the clubface open?
The face of the club should be square to your
plane and target line.

10. Is your stance open, closed, or square? It
should be square.

11. Has your backswing progressed to a position
between your shoulder and ear? If the swing
is too flat, it often causes the slice. This
is generally because you will unconsciously
correct to proceed on plane. This is asking
too much. It's too complicated and unnatural.
A flat swing affects weight transfer from your
right foot to your left and keeps your shoulders,
body, and head position from remaining square
at impact.

CURES

Now that you have analyzed your own swing, you can
consider solutions in a conscientious way.

1. You may be turning your hips to the left
too much, preventing your arms, hands, and
the clubhead from arriving in their correct
positions both at the top and at impact.

2. Be careful that your wrists are not releasing,
or unhinging, before impact instead of at impact.

3. The problem can be caused by your body swaying to the right on the backswing. Make sure your left knee points down at the ball. It should be a comfortable pivot with your right knee staying in address position. Without proper use of your legs, which is a driving motion toward the intended target, it's almost impossible to transfer weight from your right leg to your left foot and leg.

4. Finally, your shoulders should move slightly vertically—not predominantly horizontally.

Hooking

Generally, a golfer who has a hooking problem has considerably more experience than one who slices. However, it is equally important to minimize or stop hooking completely. A nice "draw," in which the ball moves in a slight right-to-left pattern, is great for most women players, but it must be consistent and free of the occasional hook. Both shots generally gain distance due to the increased roll of the ball, but a hook can destroy your game. Often, there is little or no hope of recovery.

A hook results from spinning the ball right to left excessively. In a draw, the ball spins like a hook but not as severely. Instead, the ball modestly turns right to left but remains reasonably straight. And, of course, it should leave you with a good shot. It guarantees more distance because the ball will roll upon landing.

The expert golfer generally has control and can score lower by negotiating problems such as wind, trees, or other factors that make it convenient to be able to fade or draw.

Many great women golfers prefer to execute a fade or a draw rather than hit a perfectly straight shot. A draw generally produces more roll and distance; a fade permits the ball to stop more quickly. A draw is especially helpful on long-distance shots, whereas a fade is an advantage when hitting to the green.

Most golfers who slice or hook will intentionally aim in the wrong direction hoping the ball will return to the target. For example, a slicer will aim left hoping the ball will curve to the right and hit the target. The opposite is true for a hooker who aims to the right hoping the ball will turn back left to the target.

Those who hook often do so because they are aligning their shoulders, feet, and hips to the right. They also naturally swing more inside-out than normal, compounding the problem. As a result, the shot is lower and the hook only becomes more pronounced.

CURES

1. Check your grip. Your left hand may be turned too far right. Often, the right hand is also too far to the right or even under the club. You should be able to see two knuckles of your left hand and one on your right hand.
2. Take the clubhead back on plane and not too much inside.
3. Correct your alignment. The plane should point down the target line.
4. Check your shoulders and hips. They should be parallel to, or square with, the target line.
5. Often, from the top of the swing one tries to hit the ball too early and too hard. Performed

correctly, a downswing is slow and smooth with an accelerated action through the ball.

Heeling

This shot feels horrible, and it's almost a "shank." (A shank occurs when the flight of the ball is almost a right angle to your target line.) You suffer a loss of power. The ball flies only a short distance, generally starting left and then slicing. When this happens, you haven't hit the ball in the sweet spot of the clubface; you've hit it on the heel, thereby losing power.

CURES

1. Be sure your weight remains on your heels.
2. Your right arm must remain close to your body on the downswing.

Push Shot

This is similar to a slice, but, instead of turning right, the ball simply starts to the right and continues in a straight line.

CURES

1. Most likely, you are swaying. Your head and body move to the right on the backswing, and your body cannot return to impact position in time.
2. The body sway is often due to your left heel lifting or moving too much and, as a result,

it is unable to return to address position at impact.

Skying the Ball

At one time, this was called "scaffling." It is a ball hit on the underside so that it goes at an extremely high trajectory with little distance gained.

CURES

1. Don't let your right shoulder drop on the forward swing.
2. If you are driving, try teeing the ball a little lower.
3. Don't drop your head during the swing.
4. You may be trying to hit the ball harder than normal. Be sure to keep your swing easy.

Spraying

Spraying occurs when you hit the ball in a variety of directions, and none of them are at the target. One shot goes left, and the next shot goes right. Your shots defy prediction, and you've lost control. It's simply a case of being wild.

CURES

1. Be consistent in positioning the ball at address.
2. Don't sway or move your head excessively.

Toeing

If you are hitting the ball with the toe of the clubface, you are not permitting the loft of the club to do the work.

CURES

1. Make sure that your weight isn't shifting to your heels during the swing.
2. Complete your follow-through, and be sure not to raise your head.

Topping

This is a basic flaw suffered from time to time. It's usually caused by being too anxious to hit the ball. As a result, you mis-hit the ball, never getting it airborne. It generally happens when you are trying to hit a good ball over a lake or hit an especially long shot. You become anxious to see the results. In the swing, you've probably moved your head and changed the plane. This affects the impact.

CURES

1. Keep your eyes on the ball. Professional Jim Langley says he often aims at a few dimples on the ball to prevent this problem and gain maximum impact. So keep your head steady.
2. Be sure not to raise your body prematurely. Check to see if you are crouching at address. This causes an unconscious correction during the swing by raising the body.

3. Keep your right elbow close to your body. A "flying right elbow" often causes topping.

Shanking

Unfortunately, you may be familiar with this problem. It occurs when your ball flies so suddenly and so far to the right that you can barely trace its flight. This is definitely a disease. Many professionals refuse to aid anyone with the "shanks"; they're afraid it's contagious. If I'm playing with someone who has this problem (see, I even hate to refer to the word), I won't watch them swing. I've had some experience with this affliction in my own game.

You can try to be positive. I have a friend who, when he hits a shank, exclaims, "Boy, that was one-half inch from a perfect hit!" However, in one particularly bad case, a professional hit his ball to within six feet of the green, and then proceeded to hit ten straight shanks. Each shank was at such a severe right angle to his intended target that he wasn't able to get to the green. Finally, he picked up his ball and withdrew from the tournament. Johnny Miller, when he was co-leading the Bing Crosby Tournament, suffered the shanks on the 16th hole at Pebble Beach. At the time, he had a chance to win the tournament. He, and everyone else, was shocked. His fellow competitors wouldn't even walk near him.

CURES

Now for the positive side. If you find a cure, you will thoroughly enjoy the game again. Of course, to find the cure you must *go to the practice range!*

1. Place a ruler parallel to the intended line of flight one to two inches from the ball. Practice until you no longer hit the ruler.

2. Since most shanks are on short shots, work harder on this part of your game using a ruler at all times. Be sure to stay on plane.

3. Your shoulders are probably not maintaining their position during the swing—especially your right shoulder, which would be projecting out during the swing instead of coming under the chin.

4. Check that you are not falling forward on your toes during the swing.

5. Keep your hands under your chin during the swing.

6. An exaggerated inside-outside swing is also a mysterious cause. Your inside-outside swing can be too severe and you shank—the "neck" of the club (where the clubhead joins the shaft) hits the ball instead of the clubface. The club simply does not meet the ball squarely in the center of the ball or the center of the clubface.

7. Do not rock your body or allow your head to move forward during the swing.

Always use the ruler. Consider the points listed, diagnose the problem, and you can forget all about it. One of my friends, Hal Higgins, calls this shot a lateral. I refuse to call it anything.

CROWDING THE BALL AND CLOSING THE CLUBFACE LIKE THIS CAUSES A SMOTHERED SHOT.

Smothered Shot

"Smothering" is a combination of your body crowding over the ball at impact and the clubface closing at contact. This is a disaster, but it's also rather simple to correct. I remember playing with a competitor (and I will never let him forget it) who smothered one of his drives. It hit a post left of the tee and flew over our heads one hundred yards out of bounds. Smothering ruins your game.

CURES

1. Check your grip. If your hands are too far right on the grip, the clubhead will close too early.
2. Try moving the ball forward in your stance.
3. Do not get ahead of your swing. In other words, don't move your body, head, and shoulders to the left during the downswing. Use proper hand action through impact and stay on plane.

Finally, if you have any other problems that seem especially mysterious, contact your professional. They are generally very knowledgeable and are always willing to help you.

12.

· ·

The Right Club for Every Shot

All golfers have periods of time when they aren't able to play the game, whether they've been through a severely cold winter, enjoyed a nongolfing vacation, or endured an illness. You can get yourself back into playing condition with a few simple sessions. Before these sessions, allow a little time to prepare for swinging.

Before practice or play, a series of brief stretching exercises will help you warm up. Most often, I simply swing a club in slow motion and then work up to a full swing. After five or more full swings, you're ready for the golf course.

Of course, if you live a considerable distance from your course, a few more stretching exercises and practice swings will be needed once you arrive at the practice tee.

If you plan to play golf that day, it's best not to become fatigued with practice. If you're an advanced player, you have already developed your basic game and practice will only make you more limber. Even advanced players, however, may want to correct a swing flaw, and the best place for such work is the practice tee.

One word of caution. Although you may correct a swing flaw in practice, pressure increases during actual play and you'll often revert to old habits. So, when playing, discipline yourself to repeat the corrections made on the practice tee.

Even before your home practice, warm up with a few stretching exercises. One acquaintance of mine hadn't played during Iowa's long, cold winter months. He began practicing immediately without warming up. Thirty minutes later, his left arm was entirely black and blue with bruises. His muscles weren't prepared for the force of the swing.

Putting Practice

If you have a carpet similar to a putting green, this is the place to begin. You can cut a piece of cloth about the size of a hole, purchase an inexpensive putting target, or use a glass as your target. Begin with short putts, making the exercise a personal contest. Try to make five to ten short putts in a row, then try to make five longer putts. Your goal on the longer putts is to be close to the hole.

Use the same goals when you begin to practice on a real putting green. Begin with level putts. After a satisfactory practice with level putts, begin varying your putts. Most practice greens have a series of holes. With several balls, play a game of simply putting from one hole to another.

Putting may not be the most exciting golf practice, but you must consider that, as you progress, one-half of your score will come from putting. And remember, it becomes fun to make a long or medium-length putt when playing against an opponent. Your putting success will certainly unnerve your opponents, and your status as a golfer will improve.

I have a mallet-head putter that I call "Big Red." Only rarely do I use it. However, I played in a tournament with Big Red and made every putt in sight. My opponents have never forgotten it. Now whenever I play with anyone who played with me during those four days I use Big Red, and they are instantly defeated. Some people claim they won't play with me unless I leave Big Red at home!

Chipping

Next, practice chipping onto the green. Most golf courses have practice chipping areas. Begin about twelve inches off the green on the fringe.

Most golfers prefer to use a putter for this shot. Although you'll need to strike these off-the-green putts slightly harder, you are still putting.

Now, place your ball three feet off the green. You can use various clubs, but, even if you don't use your putter, you'll still use a putting stroke. Try to select an iron with just enough loft, or pitch, to clear the fringe, land on the green, and roll to the hole. This is called a chip-and-run shot.

For a chip-and-run, use your normal golf grip instead of a putting grip. You'll use this grip for all of the clubs in your bag. Always use a club that will carry to the green and roll to the hole. (This is a basic shot and exceptions will be discussed later.)

Pitch Shots

Now, try some shots twenty to thirty yards from the green. Use a 9-iron or a wedge. You'll now begin to swing with the objective of getting the ball to stop close to the hole.

For the stroke between twenty and thirty yards, continue to use the plane as if you were putting. Refer to chapter 7 if you need to freshen up on the plane.

Mastering this stroke will easily separate you from other golfers. Using the same plane for this stroke—without taking the clubhead inside on the backswing and without a considerable follow-through—is very valuable.

Short Iron Shots

Move further back from the practice green and try the full wedge shot. This means that you'll hit the wedge with a full backswing and a full follow-through. Once you've hit some good shots with a full wedge, measure the distance you are able to hit this shot by taking steps of about one yard in length. Walk from the point you hit the ball to the point it stopped.

This is important. You're measuring the distance that you're able to hit the wedge. You'll also want to step off the yardage of your 9-iron, 8-iron, and 7-iron shots. It's generally true that the distance you hit each iron varies progressively by about ten yards. So if you hit a 7-iron 100 yards, a good distance for the average woman golfer, you'll know that you can hit an 8-iron about 90 yards, a 9-iron about 80 yards, and so on.

The distances that women hit the ball vary widely. The strongest women professionals may hit an 8-iron 140 yards, but many women may hit an 8-iron only 60 yards. If you know exactly how far you hit your irons, you'll add to your advantage.

Most practice ranges have yardage markers for just such measurements. These are usually color-coded flags. You'll find the code key on or near the driving range. You'll also find yardage markers on the course. They vary from color-coded disks to metal disks, often sprinkler heads, with the exact number of yards to the center of the green printed on them. Some courses also have highly visible 100-yard markers, such as white posts or cement blocks.

For example, let's say you find a yardage marker that indicates you're 130 yards from the hole. If you normally hit a 7-iron 100 yards, your calculation of adding ten yards per club will tell you that you need to use a 4-iron to hit the ball 130 yards.

Full Iron Shots

Your next practice will include the 9-iron, 8-iron, 7-iron, 6-iron, and 5-iron. Hitting each of these irons is different, but the execution of each shot is in the same family.

In an exhibition, the fine English professional Nick Faldo hit rapid-fire shots and dared anyone to tell him which club he was using. He swung all clubs from the 7-iron to the 3-iron, but his swing tempo was exactly the same with each club. The only difference was that the length of his swing seemingly increased with the length of each shot. This, however, is only an illusion. The longer clubs seem to go back farther, but they really don't; the longer length of the club shaft merely brings the club closer to parallel at the top of the backswing.

It was a beautiful exhibition and proved how important it is to use the same tempo for every full swing. Whether using a 7-iron or a driver, you should seek to swing at the same speed.

In golf, you'll sometimes hear the great phrase, "swing within yourself." In other words, make a comfortable swing without using excessive force. You'll gain the maximum and most consistent advantage.

However, there are times you'll be hitting a shot of an awkward distance. Perhaps you are 95 yards from the green. Do you hit an 8-iron harder, or do you hit a 7-iron a shorter distance than usual? Your best bet is to use the longer club, the 7-iron, and grip it two or three inches from the end of the grip. Swing it at your normal tempo, and you'll hit the 7-iron 5 yards shorter than normal, or 95 yards. This procedure can be used with all clubs.

Knowing how far you hit each iron or wood is valuable. You'll especially need this knowledge when playing in the wind or in heavy or wet grass.

A shot into the wind will normally shorten your distance with every club except for a short chip shot. With experience, you'll learn how wind strength influences your normal distance. As wind strength increases, the distance you can hit the shot decreases. Terminology for this condition is a "one-club" wind (rather mild), a "two-club" wind (quite brisk), or a "three-club" wind (very brisk). Therefore, if you would normally hit an 8-iron to the green, and you're hitting into a mild, or one-club, wind you'll need to hit a 7-iron to gain the appropriate distance.

The Driver

After becoming somewhat proficient and comfortable with your irons—the wedge, 9-, 8-, 7-, 6-, and 5-iron—I suggest you now begin practicing with the driver. Every part of the swing you have learned will now be applied to swinging the driver.

The old expression "drive for show, putt for dough" is arguably true. As stated in chapter 3, successful putting can break an opponent's heart. Similarly, hitting a good drive sets you up psychologically. It feels good, gives you position to attack the hole, and gives you confidence. A good drive gives you another advantage—the potential to play the hole well.

All shots are important. Although you cannot make up for a missed putt, you can make up for a poor drive.

To prepare for a good drive, you must tee the ball at the proper height. For most, the normal height is the thickness of your thumb under the ball. Tee height generally rewards you with a higher trajectory, which can help you gain extra distance on a downwind hole.

You may want to tee the ball lower if you are hitting into the wind. A low shot fights the wind, because, if you hit the ball high into the wind, its force will drastically reduce your distance. The amount of reduction depends on the wind velocity.

Here are some reminders for your practice. Always use the proper plane, tempo, length of stroke, and an accelerated follow-through. After hitting these practice drives with consistency, hit some practice shots with your 4-wood.

At this point, do not feel defeated if another golfer on the practice range hits much longer drives. During the learning stages, remember that you will eventually increase your distance.

The Problem with Fairway Woods and Long Irons

Please notice that we have skipped the 3-wood. Fairway woods and long irons require much more work and will demand exact execution of the swing.

The 4- and 5-wood are easier to hit than the 3-wood, which has a more steeply angled clubface. They're also slightly shorter in length, because the higher the club number, the shorter its shaft. The driver is the longest, and each club becomes progressively shorter all the way down to your wedge.

Of course, the major difference between using the driver and fairway woods is that you hit the latter from off the grass instead of from a tee. This means fairway woods must be swung so that the ball is hit with a slightly descending blow.

Many players are now using a 6- or 7-wood. More women, and more men, should use them. A 7-wood is the equivalent of a 4-iron, and many golfers find that the higher loft of a 7-wood makes it easier to use. Both the 6- and 7-wood are more effective when used from the rough or even from a fairway bunker.

Since the Rules of Golf limits players to fourteen clubs, many professionals carry only a driver and one other wood. This gives them room to carry a 1-iron and a 2-iron and often two wedges. It is your choice. Many golfers select their clubs for a round depending on that day's weather or to accommodate the condition or style of the course. An example of the style of a course is a hilly course that demands high shots.

If a course is extremely wet, for example, you won't get much roll. It's then more important to get distance in the air, so good players may carry higher lofted fairway woods instead of a 3-wood.

The Solution for Long Irons

This section addresses the most difficult clubs to hit and the most fun to conquer. For many golfers, the 3-wood, 1-iron,

2-iron, 3-iron, and 4-iron pose the most difficulty. I would say that the 1-iron and 2-iron are the most difficult. The 3-iron is less difficult, and, among the long irons, the 4-iron is the easiest to hit. Begin practicing with the 4-iron and, once you feel competent using it, progress to the 3-iron. They are similar shots.

After gaining confidence with the 3-iron, progress directly to the 3-wood. When you can use all of the above-mentioned clubs with confidence, you will have greatly expanded the depth of your game and be able to play with anyone.

Once you feel comfortable with the 3-wood, progress to the 2-iron. When you're confident with the 2-iron, begin using a 1-iron—if you have one. Most people, except touring professionals, don't use or even own a 1-iron. Lee Trevino once joked that when he's exposed to lightning he holds a 1-iron over his head, because even God can't hit a 1-iron!

Using a 1-, 2-, or 3-iron can be fun and will certainly improve your game. The ability to hit a long, low, running shot is important, but most golfers can't hit it with much confidence. Because they're used for such shots, long irons offer a great advantage when hitting into the wind.

On a day when you're hitting the ball well at a practice range, set the ball up on the grass and try using a driver. You don't need to spend a lot of time working on this shot, because you'll rarely use it. But when distance is required and the ball must stay low, perhaps to go under a tree limb or to advance against a very strong wind, a well-hit driver from the fairway is spectacular.

The ability to hit these more difficult shots is great fun. After many years of playing golf, I can still remember almost every good shot I made using a driver off the fairway. It always feels marvelous and leaves opponents stunned.

TO HIT THE BALL HIGH, BEGIN BY POSITIONING THE BALL FORWARD OF
THE CENTER OF YOUR STANCE.

FOR A LOW SHOT, BEGIN BY POSITIONING THE BALL BACK OF THE
CENTER OF YOUR STANCE.

High and Low Shots

If you intend to hit the ball high, attempt to hit the ball on the underside, striking the ball and the turf at the same time. To do this, play the ball forward in your stance, near your left toe. Be sure to complete your swing.

Sometimes you'll need to hit a low shot. To do so, play the ball back in your stance at address. Swing sharply down and hit the ball before you take the turf. Your hands should stay *ahead* of the clubhead. You can also close the clubface slightly at address to decrease its loft.

Before the Round

Unless you intend to use the practice range to simply work on your game, instead of for a brief warm up before a game, don't hit many shots. When warming up, your purpose is to establish tempo, rhythm, and consistency. It's not a learning process. Some people never warm up—big mistake—and others hit only ten to fifteen balls. Many golfers stop when they feel their confidence level is up. This is your primary purpose in warming up.

Time is also a factor. Try to arrive at the golf course as stress free as possible. Allow time for brief visiting and hitting a few relaxed warm-up shots.

13.

. . . .

Gimmicks, Gadgets, and Gurus

Americans, ever inventive, love gadgets, and it's no accident that "build a better mouse trap" is the premise upon which American business is built. Similarly, American golfers have joined the ranks of those looking for a more efficient method through the use of gadgets. Just look in the back of any golf magazine and you'll see a host of golf gadgets designed to improve your game with virtually no effort on your part.

I have a friend, Jack, who loves golf gadgets. His golf cart is so elaborate that it received nationwide publicity. It's equipped with a weather vane, wind machine, thermometer, heater, cooling fan, police lights, taillights, turn signals, Citizens Band radio, television, and telephone.

He has more than 4,000 putters, most of which he gives away. He also has a headband with weights to strengthen his neck muscles, a device to strengthen his wrists, a ring to check the roundness of his golf balls, and a practice swing device that records the probable distance a ball will go with each swing.

Jack assembled a twelve-inch-thick collection of copies of instruction articles from various golf magazines. After he married a woman who was willing to participate in his passion for golf, Jack gave her the book to study. Some wedding present! It took a lot of courage on her part, but she did become a proficient golfer.

A friend of mine from Germany asked me to help him learn to play golf. He became so enthused that he installed a practice net and driving mat in his garage. His neighbors became alarmed by the noise of his practice sessions that, rather than ask him about it, they called the police to investigate.

Many of us have a favorite accessory to help improve our game. I personally use a gadget for strengthening my wrists. Be cautious when purchasing golf gadgets. One company sold a saline solution with the sales pitch that by placing the golf ball in the solution you could discover its center of gravity. Then, by marking your ball at the proper point, you could hit it on that spot and get a better shot. Such innovations are simply a waste of money and some of them are illegal by the USGA's equipment standards. Clubs with adjustable parts and special gadgets for checking yardage and wind direction are not approved for use during play.

Some training devices, however, can help you improve your swing. One such device is the Perfect Swing Trainer, marketed by professional Peter Kostis. In my opinion, it's an asset for any teaching professional, but it is an expensive aid for the average golfer. It is a circular device made of steel. It's adjustable to fit each golfer's stature. The Perfect Swing Trainer can aid "muscle memory" in learning both the backswing and the forward swing on the proper plane. One teaching professional claims that his students improve four times faster by using this device. Of course, students must be dedicated to improvement and work diligently on their games.

So-called "gurus" enjoy popularity in many sports, and in recent years they've found golf to be a fertile field for their theories. Golf gurus range from teaching professionals with sophisticated techniques to sports psychologists.

One professional was shooting average scores of around seventy, and one of his playing companions averaged about seventy-four strokes per round. A sports psychologist told them that he could help them improve their scores by four strokes each. The two golfers signed up, and the sports psychologist guaranteed his work. He said if they weren't satisfied, they wouldn't have to pay. One month later, his friend shot a seventy. The golf professional, however, lost his game entirely, and it took several months and much mental anguish for him to recover.

Can you imagine someone trying to aid the mental processes of Jack Nicklaus or Nancy Lopez? Although we can't classify them as geniuses, they sure know how to play winning golf. Good golf simply takes persistence and hard knocks, and golfers who lean on someone to straighten out their mental processes will eventually fail.

A sports psychologist can study attitudes, development, procedures, and individual personalities. All of these are interesting to analyze, but golf is a game of self-reliance. It takes natural ability, training, and hard work to play well. In golf, you must establish muscle memory and learn to analyze a course hole by hole. I can hardly imagine a beginning golfer, or even an average player, spending money on a therapist when she could make the same gains by taking lessons and engaging in diligent practice.

14.

. . . .

Golf Etiquette

There is an age-old code of behavior on the golf course that is designed to give each player the *opportunity* to play her best shot. Although golf etiquette is defined in the Rules of Golf, there are no penalties for infractions. Golfers who frequently breach golf etiquette, however, will find that they soon alienate other players and will probably have some difficulty in getting other people to play with them.

Golf etiquette is outlined in this chapter, and it's easy to observe this code if you simply remember to be courteous to other players, including those who will be playing the course later in the day.

Some points of golf etiquette are also designed for safety,

such as where to stand when another golfer is playing a stroke. When a golfer is playing a stroke, your objective is to avoid interfering with the shot. Always stand far enough away from another player's ball so that she will not see you when she is making a stroke. Stand on the opposite side of the ball from the golfer and slightly behind her. Do not stand forward of the ball. We all intend to hit a straight shot, but we all occasionally miss a shot. Remember, the ball can fly any direction but backwards. Don't stand directly to the player's right behind the ball. Most of us have fairly good peripheral vision and can be distracted by someone standing directly behind our ball.

Always remain silent when someone else is playing a stroke. Stand quietly. Don't make practice swings or rattle your equipment. Golf is a quiet game and noises are very distracting to a player who is trying to concentrate on making a stroke.

When another player is on the tee, don't stand on the teeing area. Stand away from the tee markers.

Do not hit your ball until the group of golfers in front of you is safely out of reach. Never hit to a green still occupied by golfers. Wait until they have left the green and are well past it as they proceed to the next tee.

If you accidentally hit a ball that endangers another player, yell "fore!" as quickly and loudly as you can. This is a universal warning to all golfers that a ball in flight is approaching them. This is an important safety point to remember.

Order of Play

The player with the lowest score on the previous hole has the "honor" on the next tee and tees off first. (If there is a tie on the previous hole, the player who had the honor on that hole retains it.) The player with the next lowest score on the previous hole tees off next, and so on. On the first tee, the order of play can be decided by lot, mutual agreement, or a flip of the coin.

Other than on the tee, the player who is farthest from the hole is said to be "away," and she plays first. This order of play applies on the fairway and the putting green.

Interference

If your ball will interfere with another player's stroke on the fairway, the player may ask you to mark the ball's position with a small coin or ball marker and lift it. You are not allowed to clean your ball under these circumstances. After the player has made her stroke, replace your ball.

On the putting green, if your ball will interfere with another player's stroke or if it is in her line of vision and will distract her, mark your ball and lift it. You are allowed to clean your ball after you have lifted it on the putting green. When it is your turn to play, replace your ball.

Never leave your clubs or equipment in an area around another player's ball or on the tee, fairway, or putting green. Even a carelessly thrown towel lying on the green can be very distracting to another player.

Scoring

After completing a hole, immediately report your score for the hole to the player who is keeping the scorecard. If you are keeping the scorecard, be sure to record all scores before teeing off on the next hole.

Care of the Course

Do not damage the course. If you take a divot, replace the turf after you have completed your stroke. Do not take divots on practice swings.

Don't walk through bunkers or place your clubs in bunkers. Be sure to repair any damage you make when playing a shot from the bunker. A rake is provided for this purpose. After you have played a stroke from a bunker, rake the sand until it is smooth again. Be sure to rake any footprints you make as you leave the bunker. Always enter and exit a bunker from the side or back of the bunker. Never climb up the steep face of the bunker, unless that is the location of your ball and you must stand in the face of the bunker to play your stroke.

Never pull a pull cart onto the tee or green. Keep all pull carts at least ten yards from tees, greens, and bunkers.

Don't place your golf bag on the green. Place your clubs gently to the side of the green, tee, or bunker.

When you remove a flagstick from the hole, never toss it on the green because it will damage the putting surface. Lay the flagstick off the side of the green, or lay it gently on the putting surface far enough from any ball that it will not interfere with play.

If the impact of your ball makes a mark on the green, called a "ball mark," repair the mark by pushing the pointed end of a golf tee under the damaged grass. Slightly raise the grass with the tee until the grass is level, and tamp down the grass with the head of your putter.

Slow Play

Don't rush your game, but play as quickly as you can. If you and your group have paused to look for a lost ball, turn to the group playing behind you and wave them through. If they choose to "play through," stand quietly and wait until they are well out of the way before playing the next shot.

If there are one or more vacant holes ahead of you, signal to the group playing behind you to play through.

Upon completing play of a hole, don't stand on the putting green to discuss play or record your score. Leave the green immediately so that the next group can continue play.

If you follow these simple points, you'll be welcome with any group of golfers.

15.

Exercising for Golf

Most of us know that an exercise
program improves both our health and sense of well-being.
Today's professionals also acknowledge that exercise can be of
great benefit to our golf game. Exercises geared for our golf needs
not only add strength but are also ideal for improving flexibility
and endurance.

In this chapter, I'll cover exercises to improve your game.
Over the years, I've worked out an exercise program, with the
help of doctors, that is beneficial to my health and my golf game.
Other benefits of this program include an improved cardiovascu-
lar system, better muscle tone, gradual weight loss, a slowed ag-
ing process, improved back problems, and a firmer stomach. Try
it and you'll be pleasantly surprised at the results.

This is a home exercise program, so you won't need to buy expensive machines or visit physical fitness centers. Your goals in golf will influence the amount of exercise you do—so will your age, condition, physical ability, and desire. Before beginning any exercise program, visit your doctor or cardiologist to determine your own work-out standards and maximum pulse rate.

All exercise should have a time limit, increased only by adding other exercises. Our program will be much like a school curriculum, and we'll start with three classes weekly: stretching, muscle toning, and electives. Although three sessions a week is adequate, six sessions can be exhilarating and far more effective.

Electives

One elective a week is enough. You may choose to alternate these days with your stretching exercise days, although I like to perform all exercises during one period a day. The electives include brisk walking, jogging, aerobics classes, dancing, swimming, bicycling (including stationary), rowing, wrist exercises, and toe touching.

Electives can be alternated. If you're interested in the stationary bicycle, it's not necessary to buy an elaborate model. Mine cost approximately $100 and has a speedometer, a dial for making the bicycle more difficult to pedal, and a timer. Other than a good fit, that's all you need. Stationary bikes that monitor your pulse, blood pressure, and that have other additions are expensive and won't add any real benefits.

A good way to start is by doing the stretch exercises six days a week and walking three days a week weather permitting. Medical research shows that a forty-minute walk three times a week has great health benefits. Additional walking adds only minimal benefits.

Jogging isn't for everyone. It can cause foot and knee injuries. The same is true for aerobics. Swimming is a great exercise, but it's not for everyone. Dancing is a lot of fun, builds stamina, and is an excellent aerobic exercise. Dancing three times a week, however, is generally impractical unless you're in a dance class.

Walking can be very enjoyable. On a personal note, I had a long layoff due to health problems. As I recovered, I began walking ⅙ mile per day. The walk was slow, but within a few weeks I had gradually increased the walk to four miles a day and finally to seven miles a day. Today's busy schedules prohibit such time-consuming walks, so I now consider a one-hour walk a day adequate.

I read recently about a woman who began doing a one-mile walk in forty minutes. A few weeks later, she was able to walk two miles in forty minutes. A good goal after a few weeks is to increase your walking speed until you're capable of walking one mile in fifteen minutes.

Stretching

Here is a brief limbering sequence: one minute of stretching, followed by four minutes of muscle toning, followed by five minutes of nonstop activity to raise your heart rate. We'll use only four stretching exercises.

1. First, try to balance on your toes and raise one arm as high as possible. Reach for the sky! Then change to the other arm and repeat.

Count to fifteen slowly or watch a clock for fifteen seconds.

2. Turn and reach to one side as far as possible with both arms and hands, turning your body in the same direction. Now turn, not snap, your body and arms in the other direction. Continue for fifteen seconds.

3. Bend over and grasp your legs behind your knees. Now, pull your shoulders toward your knees, pulling them as far as you can without straining. Hold this position for fifteen seconds.

4. Limber your neck. Without jerking your head, turn it left as far as possible and then right as far as possible. Continue for fifteen seconds.

Muscle Toning

The next phase develops muscle. Begin slowly and, in a short time, increase the movement. This series involves three exercises: pushaways, sitbacks, and the imaginary club swing.

PUSHAWAYS

Instead of pushups, which take tremendous upper body strength, do pushaways. Begin by standing facing a wall with your arms extended and your hands against the wall at shoulder height. Lean into the wall and push back until you are standing erect. Then, permit your body to return to the wall.

Repeat 15 to 20 times. As it becomes easier, stand farther from the wall. Soon you can place your hands on a counter, push back, and return.

Your goal is a set of 20 to 25 repetitions. After a breather, repeat your last sequence 20 to 25 times. You should find it becoming easier. You can proceed progressively to a lower table or chair.

SITBACKS

Situps are too stressful, so we'll do sitbacks. This is great for your abdominal muscles. Have someone hold onto your feet or secure them under a heavy piece of furniture such as a couch. Flex your knees when you sit down and place your chest near your knees. Now place your hands on your abdomen. Lean back as far as you can without going all the way to the floor. At first, you won't be able to go very far. Inhale before leaning back and exhale as you lean back and hold that position. Once you've leaned back several inches, hold it for 15 to 20 seconds. If you've gone back too far, relax, let yourself go to the floor, and try again.

In a few weeks, your strength will improve. When you progress almost to the floor and return, add some difficulty by crossing your arms over your chest. Always rest and check your pulse. If your pulse is okay, repeat the exercise.

IMAGINARY CLUB SWING

Here is a brief exercise that I firmly believe will help your golf game, and you don't have to pick up a club. Act as if you have a club in your hands and stand the appropriate distance from a line of the floor.

Without a club, take a short backswing and a short follow-through. The follow-through should accelerate but not be vicious or overactive. It's as if you are chipping the ball. Check to be sure that your hands are in the proper position. Your head remains still, your shoulders come under your chin, and you should try for the true timing of a golf swing. Do this four to six times. Then add length to your take-away and follow-through.

Do your hands move freely? Have you kept your head still on the follow-through? Is your follow-through of an equal length to your backswing? Are you accelerating?

Do this exercise five or six times. Now take the "club" back halfway or a little more than halfway. Hit the imaginary ball with a little acceleration and an equal follow-through. Are your shoulders moving under your chin and is your head remaining still? Repeat this four to six times.

Take the imaginary club back in a three-quarter swing. Are your knees moving in the correct way? Is your right knee staying in place with your left knee moving toward your right knee? For pace, you should feel an acceleration through the imaginary ball. Repeat this five or six times.

Now, it's time for a full swing. Take the club back to parallel. Have your hands reacted so that the clubface would be directly vertical? Are your knees in proper position?

Begin your accelerated swing through the ball. Hit through the ball, staying low during the follow-through until your right knee is moving toward your left knee and your follow-through is complete with your hands above your shoulders.

During this swing, has your head stayed behind the ball? Do this five to ten times until you feel you have developed a perfect imaginary swing.

Please be assured that this will help your golf game immensely. You are developing "muscle memory." The only thing different on the golf course is that you must be able to find the ball's sweet spot and contact it with the clubhead.

A second version involves a training club. They weigh considerably more than regular golf clubs and several companies sell them. Advocates believe practice with the weighted club gives golfers added flexibility. You can also use a round plastic weighted device, called a "donut," that fits over your club shaft close to the clubhead. This weight has much the same effect and will give you similar results. These plastic donuts are inexpensive and easy to find in golf shops.

Several pros advocate using a training club with an ultra-whippy shaft, which is almost like a rubber shaft. Any slight movement of the shaft will move the clubhead three feet or so. I have some close friends, professionals in Southern California, who value this training technique. They believe golfers can develop a better feel for the location of the clubhead throughout the swing, and they interpret this as extremely important to educating your hands.

One friend of mine owns an entire set and uses them while playing. He's an older gentleman and doesn't swing hard, yet he gains acceptable distance using these clubs. But I don't encourage you to use these clubs while playing. I'm simply exposing you to several types of practice clubs.

After this series of exercises, you may want to choose an elective. After about twenty minues, check your pulse rate. If it's okay, feel free to continue with any exercise you would like to repeat or begin.

All of these exercises are simple and quick. From here, you may want to do more than just one elective a week.

16.

A Brief Review

Now that you've absorbed knowl-
edge and achieved reasonable efficiency, remember that the time
you spend in practice and play will help you develop your game.
You can now establish goals and seek to improve your game as
you raise your goals.

In the near future, you should read the Rules of Golf. It
may seem heavy going, but the Rules can help your game and
knowing them will make you a more complete golfer. Pick up a
copy of Tom Watson's *The Rules of Golf Illustrated and Explained*.
It will help you understand the Rules through its excellent illus-
trations and explanations.

Now that you've advanced, analyze your game after each

round. Were you dissatisfied with some of your shots? Was your round a disaster? Did you consistently repeat your errors?

Refer to this book from time to time for a review of your swing and common problems you may have with your game. Try to analyze the cures as well as the faults.

Everyone seems to have recurring problems in golf, because we repeat our mistakes. After many years of playing golf, I wrote a letter to myself about my most common problems and how to solve them. I ended up with a list of twelve problems I often encounter in my game and the cures I can use to solve them.

See your golf professional for an occasional checkup. Professionals are trained to find flaws that you cannot feel. Your professional can become your most trusted adviser.

Remember to be patient with yourself. Bobby Jones observed that no one has ever played a perfect round of golf. Jack Nicklaus echoed that thought, saying that every golfer who has ever broken a scoring record has claimed that there were a few missed shots that could have led to an even more phenomenal score.

When Al Geiberger scored a record 59 on eighteen holes, the players in his group claimed that he missed four or five shots. This is an important lesson. A good golf round is not necessarily made up of perfect shots. Every round consists of a number of shots that were no more than good misses. Therefore, your game depends not only on good shots but also on good misses.

Let's review some of the important points you've learned in this book.

1. Always make sure that you have a good grip
    and stance and proper ball position.

2. Use the pressure points of your grip.

3. Carefully choose your plane.

4. Your left shoulder should move under your chin on the backswing—your right shoulder under your chin on the forward swing.

5. Do not sway.

6. Don't raise your body or head during the swing.

7. Keep your swing simple, and don't allow your wrists to dip or the clubhead to pass the horizontal line at the top of your backswing.

8. Check the movement of your legs. On the backswing, your right knee remains in position, slightly bent, and becomes a pivot point. Your left knee pivots toward your right knee on the take-away. On the forward swing, your right knee moves forward so that your hips, chest, shoulders, and head face the target at the end of the swing; your left knee, heel, and foot return to address position.

9. Keep your swing smooth but firm.

10. Always accelerate on your forward swing, whether you're putting or hitting a full shot.

11. On the forward swing, your head and left side should not move beyond the area in which the clubhead strikes the ball.

12. Play your own game, but have fun and take time to smell the flowers!

Glossary of Golf Terms and Phrases

acceleration—the increasing speed of the downswing

address—establishing your stance, posture, and ball position

away—The player whose ball is farthest from the hole and who hits first is said to be away.·

back nine—holes ten through eighteen on an eighteen-hole course

backspin—the spin that makes the ball stop quickly

backswing—the first half of the swing in which the club travels from address position to the top of the swing

back tees—the set of tee markers farthest back in the tee area

ball mark—a mark made on a green by the impact of the ball

ball marker—a small, round marker that is used to mark your ball's location on the green so that another player may putt

ball position—the location of the ball in your stance

Band-Aid—a temporary solution to a problem

birdie—a score of one stroke under par on a hole

blade putter—a style of putters with extremely narrow heads

bogey—a score of one stroke over par on a hole, a double bogey is two strokes over, a triple bogey is three strokes over, etc.

break—the direction a putt rolls on the green

bunker—a hollow filled with sand, *also called a sand trap*

chip—a short shot onto the green, usually a running shot

chipping green—a green for practicing chip shots

clearing the left hip—turning the hip left after impact

clearing your left side—turning to the left after impact

closed clubface—the clubface is turned to the left of the target line

closed stance—the right foot is pulled back from a line that is perpendicular to the target line

clubface—the front of the clubhead that contacts the ball

clubhead—the heavy, round end of the club which strikes the ball

clubhead speed—the velocity of the clubhead

divot—a piece of turf removed from the ground by the impact of the clubhead

donut—a round, plastic weight that fits over the club shaft for practice

draw—when the ball moves in a slight right-to-left pattern

driver—the club used to hit the ball from the tee on most holes, often marked with the number "1"

eagle—a score of two strokes under par on a hole

equator—the middle of the ball

fading—making the ball travel in a slight left-to-right pattern

fairway—the smoothly cut stretch of grass between the tee and the green

fairway bunker—a bunker located in the fairway

fairway woods—the 3-, 4-, and 5-woods

fat shot—a shot resulting from the clubhead striking the ground before striking the ball.

flange—on a sand wedge, the wide bottom of the clubhead

flex—the amount of bend in a shaft

follow-through—the second half of the swing from impact with the ball to the completion of the swing

forward tees—the first set of tee markers, formerly called the ladies' tees

fried egg—a ball that is half buried in the sand

fringe—the short grass around the green that is slightly longer than the grass on the green

front nine—holes one through nine on an eighteen-hole course

golf bag—the bag used to carry clubs, tees, balls, and any other items needed on the course

golf glove—a leather or synthetic glove that provides a better grip on the club

golf shoes—shoes with spiked soles that are specifically designed to provide traction for golfers as they swing

golf shop—a shop staffed by golf professionals where you can your pay fees and buy golf equipment, *also called the pro shop*

golf umbrella—an over-sized umbrella for use on the golf course

green—the area of extremely well-manicured grass on which the hole is located

greens fee—the fee paid to play a round of golf

greenside bunker—a bunker next to a green

grip—both the name of the rubber or leather part of the club that you hold and the way you place your hands on the club

handicap—the average number over par that you usually score, a differential with par

headcovers—cloth covers that are placed over the heads of woods to protect them

heel—the part of the clubhead closest to the shaft

heeling—when the heel of the clubhead strikes the ball, causing it to fly only a short distance

hitting from the top—an incorrect downswing, in which the hands move first instead of the body

hitting under the ball—hitting below the equator of the ball

honor—A player has the honor on a hole if she had the lowest score on the previous hole. This means she tees off first.

hooking—a ball curving abruptly to the left

impact—the moment at which the clubhead meets the ball

irons—The clubs numbered one through nine with thin, knife-like clubheads; they are used for accuracy.

line of a putt—the imaginary line from the ball to the hole on which your putt should roll

loft—the degree of slope of the clubface

long irons—the 1-, 2-, and 3-irons

mallet putters—a style of putter that has a thick head

middle irons—the 4-, 5-, and 6-irons, which hit the ball a medium distance

middle tees—the set of tee markers in the middle of the teeing area, formerly called the men's tees

motorized golf cart—the electric or gas-powered cart that carries two players and their clubs around the course

nine—Every golf course is laid out in groups of nine holes. For example, an eighteen-hole course consists of two nines.

open clubface—when the clubface is turned to the right

open stance—when the right foot is in front of a line that is perpendicular to the target line

out-of-bounds stakes—white stakes that mark the outer limits of the course; instead of stakes, there may be a white out-of-bounds line

over-spin—Caused by hitting the ball with the putter head traveling slightly up, this allows the ball to stay on line.

par—the number of strokes in which a hole is designed to be played

pin placement—the location of the flagstick on the green

pitching wedge—an iron with greater loft than the 9-iron used for short shots to the green

plane—an imaginary line from the beginning of the backswing al the way to the top of the backswing and forward to the completion of the follow-through, *also called the line*

playing through—one group of golfers playing a hole while the group ahead of them waits

practice bunker—a bunker adjacent to a chipping green from which to practice sand shots

practice putting green—a green on which to practice putting

practice tee—an area for practicing full shots, *also called the driving range*

pull cart—a cart with wheels on which the walking golfer transports a set of clubs

pulling the trigger—beginning the downswing

pushed shot—a shot that starts to the right and continues to the right in a straight line

putter—used on the green, the club with a nearly vertical clubface

putter head—the clubhead of the putter

reading the green—analyzing which way a putt will break

release—the unlocking of the wrists just prior to impact

rough—extremely long grass along the fairway and around the green

round, a—eighteen holes of golf

Rules of Golf, the—governing rules of the game that are compiled by the USGA in conjunction with the Royal and Ancient Golf Club of St. Andrews, Scotland

sand wedge—The iron with the highest loft, it has a heavy clubhead and is used for hitting out of the sand.

scorecard—A card on which to record scores, it provides the length of the holes from each tee to the center of the green; they usually feature a picture of the layout of each hole.

shaft—the long part of the club between the grip and the clubhead

shank—This occurs when the flight of the ball is almost at a right angle to the target line.

short irons—the 7-, 8-, and 9-irons and the pitching wedge, which hit the ball a short distance

skying the ball—hitting the ball on the underside so that it goes extremely high and gains little distance

slice—making the ball curve to the right

smothered shot—a combination of your body crowding over the ball at impact and the clubface closing at contact

sole—the bottom of the clubhead

spraying—hitting the ball in various directions, none of which are your target

stance—the position of the feet at address

standing up to the ball—establishing the stance

take-away—the first part of the backswing

target—the spot at which you are aiming your shot

tee—the closely clipped area of grass from which play on each hole begins

tee markers—the sets of markers that designate the various tees

tee time—the scheduled time at which to begin playing a round

tempo—the transfer of power from the backswing to the downswing

thin shot—This mishit occurs when the clubface strikes above the ball's center.

timing—connecting the individual components of the swing

toe—the part of the clubface farthest from the shaft

toeing—hitting the ball with the toe of the clubface

topping—hitting the ball above its center

torque—the twist of a club shaft

turn, the—the continuation of play from the front nine to the back nine

water hazard—any body of water (lake, sea, pond, river, or ditch) on a golf course

woods—The clubs numbered one through five with massive clubheads used for distance, woods may be numbered as high as fifteen, but this is unusual.

yardage marker—On the driving range, it's a marker, usually a color-coded flag, that allows you to determine how far you are hitting the ball. On the course, they are disks or stakes used to mark the distance to the center of the green.

About the Authors

VERN JUERGENS, a resident of Carmel, California, has developed a reputation in the Midwest and California as an outstanding golf instructor. He has taught hundreds of junior, women, and college golfers the fundamentals of developing a good golf swing, and his students frequently return for "tune-ups."

The Juergenses truly enjoy golf as a family. One daughter is a golf professional and another daughter was an outstanding amateur but now plays very little. Vern and his wife, Marcia, are active in national golf circles and established many of the primary golf vacation tours.

RHONDA GLENN is a noted golf writer and broadcaster. Her books include, *The Junior Golf Book*, *Kathy Whitworth's Golf for Women*, and *The Illustrated History of Women's Golf*, which won the United States Golf Association's 1992 International Book Award. She lives in Trophy Club, Texas.